CAN ADA WEST

ROCKY MOUNTAINS
VANCOUVER

**Travel with Marco Polo
Insider Tips**

INSIDER TIP
**Your shortcut
to a great
experience**

MARCO POLO
TOP HIGHLIGHTS

PRINCE OF WHALES ⭐
Having the opportunity to see killer whales in their natural habitat is one of life's true adventures, made possible on a whale-watching tour in Telegraph Cove.
📷 *Tip: When the whales are close to the boat, the best view is from the top deck.*

➤ p. 63, Vancouver Island

CANADA PLACE ⭐
Sunlight and sky reflecting on the water surface, green mountains, yachts and seaplanes taking off: the promenade from the cruise pier looking west offers fabulous views.

➤ p. 42, Vancouver

INNER HARBOUR ⭐
This bay lined with yachts provides Western Canada's most beautiful backdrop, featuring the harbour and historical buildings.

➤ p. 54, Vancouver Island

PACIFIC RIM NATIONAL PARK ⭐
Rainforest, wild ocean and long beaches covered in driftwood: a magnificent national park on Canada's west coast including bears and whales (photo).

➤ p. 58, Vancouver Island

FORT ST JAMES ⭐
Once the main base for fur traders, today Fort St James is a museum village in the far north of the Yellowhead Region.
📷 *Tip: The trappers' store is a good place for a selfie.*

➤ p. 81, British Columbia

ICEFIELDS PARKWAY 6

The ideal location for admiring the panorama along the glacier road between Banff and Jasper and possibly for spotting bears and mountain goats.

📷 *Tip: Selfies come out best above the bright blue Peyto Lake.*

➤ p. 88, Rocky Mountains

WATERTON SHORELINE CRUISES 7

This cruise in the Waterton Lakes National Park offers breathtaking mountain views.

📷 *Tip: Mid-morning light is ideal for viewing the high peaks in the west.*

➤ p. 99, Rocky Mountains

ROYAL TYRRELL MUSEUM 8

A return to primeval times: in Drumheller you can experience a spectacular dinosaur display.

➤ p. 111, Alberta

DAWSON CITY 9

This well-known small town on the Klondike River was the location of the legendary gold rush of 1898.

📷 *Tip: You get a great perspective of the place from the boardwalk at river level.*

➤ p. 123, Yukon

CALGARY STAMPEDE 10

Tough guys and wild horses: the world's biggest rodeo attracts professional cowboys from as far away as Australia.

➤ p. 106, Alberta

CONTENTS

NORTHERN TERRITORIES

BRITISH COLUMBIA

ALBERTA

ROCKY MOUNTAINS

VANCOUVER ISLAND

VANCOUVER

CONTENTS

⊙   Plan your visit

€ - €€€   Price categories

(*)   Call charges apply

🍴   Eating/drinking

👜   Shopping

🍸   Going out

⛱   Top beaches

🌂   Rainy day activities

🦅   Budget activities

👪   Family activities

🚩   Classic experiences

(🗺 A2) Refers to the removable pull-out map
(🗺 a2) Refers to the inset street map on the pull-out map
(0) Located off the map

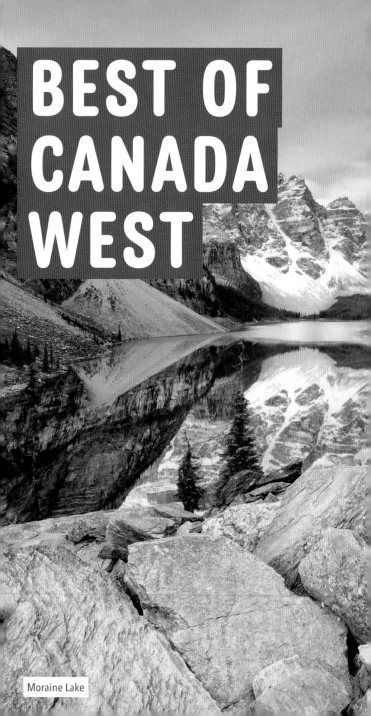

BEST OF
CANADA
WEST

Moraine Lake

BEST ☂

WHEN IT RAINS

ACTIVITIES TO BRIGHTEN YOUR DAY

UNDERWATER IN THE VANCOUVER AQUARIUM

Spend a rainy day in the large, well-designed *Vancouver Aquarium*, where you can watch animals like sea otters and fur seals.

➤ p. 42, Vancouver

A RAINFOREST IN THE RAIN

It often rains in the *Pacific Rim National Park* (photo) on the west coast of Vancouver Island. Whales and bears are not disturbed by the wet – and hopefully you won't be either.

➤ p. 58, Vancouver Island

TAKE A FERRY RIDE UP THE COAST

Dark pine forests, blue fjords, leaping orcas: on a trip through the *Inside Passage* you can sit high and dry and watch the mystical, misty fjord pass by outside.

➤ p. 62, Vancouver Island

OUTLET SHOPPING IN CALGARY

Shopping is cheap in *Crossiron Mills* in Calgary, the largest indoor discount mall in Canada. Some 200 shops offer everything from stilettos to Stetsons.

➤ p. 109, Alberta

DROWN YOUR SORROWS IN THE RANCHMAN'S SALOON

Your bad-weather blues will disappear with beer, tasty ribs and country songs in the *Ranchman's Saloon* in Calgary.

➤ p. 110, Alberta

DINOSAURS IN DRUMHELLER

Take refuge from a storm in Drumheller's *Royal Tyrrell Museum*. The bonus: when it rains, the fossil beds are laid bare – perhaps you will discover a new type of dinosaur.

➤ p. 111, Alberta

![BEST ON A BUDGET FOR SMALLER WALLETS — DOWNTOWN HOTEL]

SALMON VIEWING IN VANCOUVER

Instead of going to an aquarium, you can see wild salmon up close and for free at the *Capilano Salmon Hatchery* in the summer. Watch the fish fight against the current through large underwater observation windows.

➤ p. 45, Vancouver

CLIFF HIKING

Landscaped and paved trails are few and far between on the west coast. The *Wild Pacific Trail* in Ucluelet is free and truly stunning. Start with the Lighthouse Loop section!

➤ p. 61, Vancouver Island

THE SOUND OF THE MOUNTAINS

Enjoy jazz, classical music, dance and even opera – for free or very little money – throughout the summer at the prestigious *Banff Centre*. In August there's a three-week jazz festival, set against the magnificent mountain scenery of the Banff National Park. *banffcentre.ca*

➤ p. 92, Rocky Mountains

SUNNY MOUNTAINS, DIZZYING HEIGHTS

Whereas national parks charge admission, provincial parks in Alberta, such as *Kananaskis Country*, are free. The Rocky Mountains here are just as beautiful as in Banff but much sunnier, because it is on the eastern slopes of the mountains.

➤ p. 93, Rocky Mountains

GOLD RUSH TOWN

Historic *Dawson City*, an authentic gold rush town established in 1898, offers wonderful photo opportunities and plenty of pioneer flair (see photo) without any entrance fee.

➤ p. 123, Northern Territories

BEST

WITH CHILDREN

FUN FOR YOUNG & OLD

GRANVILLE ISLAND KIDS MARKET

A whole warehouse full of toys: everything and anything for children, from teddy bears to lunar rockets.

➤ p. 44, Vancouver

TUBING

A different way of having fun in the water is on offer at Penticton: you can drift 7km down the wide *Penticton Channel* on inflated tubes and rafts.

➤ p. 74, British Columbia

FIRST NATIONS

What does a genuine teepee or the chief's headdress look like? The *Buffalo Nations Luxton Museum* on the opposite bank of the Bow River in Banff is ideal for children: well-designed and with plenty of hands-on activities such as learning to make a bow and arrow.

➤ p. 90, Rocky Mountains

ALBERTA BIRDS OF PREY CENTRE

A sanctuary for birds of prey where injured hawks, owls and eagles are nursed back to health. Frequent flying demonstrations allow you to get close up to these magnificent creatures.

➤ p. 113, Alberta

LOOKING FOR DINOSAURS

An adventure playground for dinosaur lovers: discover extremely realistic beasts on woodland tracks in the *Jurassic Forest* near Edmonton, but beware: are they alive after all?

➤ p. 116, Alberta

HIRE A MOTORHOME

Travelling in an RV or motorhome is very popular: the vehicle creates a familiar, consistent environment while the outdoors and camping offer real adventure with wildlife watching, fishing and barbecues in the evening.

BEST 🚩

CLASSIC EXPERIENCES

ONLY IN WESTERN CANADA

SMOKED SALMON IN VANCOUVER

At the Granville Island *Public Market* you can sample the culinary treasures of Canada's west coast: raspberries, halibut and the best smoked salmon in the world.

➤ p. 46, Vancouver

ORCA WATCHING

Although the boats are not supposed to get closer than 100m to the whales, the inquisitive creatures often come closer. You may experience this on a whale-watching tour in Victoria.

➤ p. 55, Vancouver Island

CELEBRATE WITH LUMBERJACKS

It doesn't get more Canadian than the *Salmon Festival* in Campbell River, which celebrates salmon and lumberjacks – with axe throwing and bowsaw competitions.

➤ p. 61, Vancouver Island

TRAPPER FOR A DAY

Deep in the wilderness of British Columbia the wooden stockades and beaver pelts of the *Fort St James National Historic Site* take you back to the era of the fur trade.

➤ p. 81, British Columbia

LAKE VIEWS IN THE ROCKY MOUNTAINS

The view from windy *Bow Summit Pass* over the strikingly turquoise Peyto Lake is one of the most impressive sights in the Rockies (photo).

➤ p. 88, Rocky Mountains

DRIVING TO THE ARCTIC OCEAN

The trip on Canada's 700-km *Dempster Highway* takes two days and runs through the wilderness from Dawson City across the Arctic Circle towards the polar sea.

➤ p. 124, Northern Territories

GET TO KNOW CANADA WEST

Dolphins off Vancouver Island

DISCOVER CANADA WEST

Calgary's amazing skyline is mirrored on the façade of the newly constructed Bow Tower

In an ever more crowded world, Canada, with its abundance of space and wild nature is the ideal place for outdoor enthusiasts to live the dream: watch a family of bears on the shores of a fjord, enjoy the silence of the mighty Yukon River, camp with cowboys in the vastness of the prairies or go rafting through wild river rapids.

NATURE IN ABUNDANCE

Somehow people believe that they know Canada. It lies on the same latitude as central Europe, the climate is not much different from that of Europe, the

Around 15,000 BCE
Paleoamerican hunters and gatherers migrate across the Bering Strait to North America

1535/1536
Frenchman Jacques Cartier explores the St Lawrence River and first uses the name Canada

1867
The British North America Act declares the colonies of Ontario, Québec, Nova Scotia and New Brunswick to be the *Dominion of Canada*

1885
Completion of the Canada Pacific Railway line. Banff, the first Canadian National Park, is established

1898
Gold rush at Klondike.

mountains are reminiscent of the Alps, the coasts resemble those of Norway. And yet, Western Canada is completely different: huge, epic, impressive, lonely. Instead of people, noisy motorways and urban sprawl, there is an unending and vast expanse of nature, and almost every hike up to a mountain summit is rewarded with a panoramic view of a pristine landscape.

You will have to get used to Canada's dimensions. You could fit France and Germany into the province of British Columbia alone. For a first trip to Canada the western part, with its varied landscapes, is the ideal destination. On the fjord-dotted Pacific coast, the glacier-crowned Coast Mountains, with their ancient and mysterious rain forests, rise up from the dark waters, the habitat of whales and king salmon. Behind the mountains lie sunny plateaus rich in forests and lakes – interspersed with mountain ranges – that extend out as far as the Rocky Mountains. The Rockies have the most beautiful national parks in the country, Banff and Jasper, which are connected by the Icefields Parkway, a spectacular scenic road.

CATTLE AND OIL

Even further eastwards, beyond the Rockies, is the ranch country of Alberta, where dinosaurs once roamed, as evidenced by the rich fossil finds along the Red Deer River. Today, large herds of cattle graze there – in a bizarre coexistence

Oil discovered in Alberta

1931
Canada becomes a sovereign state in the Commonwealth

1962
Completion of the Trans-Canada Highway

1990s
A wave of immigration from Hong Kong brings 70,000 Chinese to Vancouver

2010
Winter Olympic Games in Vancouver

2017
Huge fires in British Columbia destroy over 25,000km² of forest

2018
Cannabis use legalised

with the oil pumps that extract Alberta's black gold. Thanks to the huge deposits of tar sands around Fort McMurray, Canada in fact has the second largest oil reserves in the world, after Saudi Arabia. Both the oil fields and the large wheat fields in the southern part of the region are evidence of the economy's dependence on the country's abundant natural resources.

THE TERRITORIES TO THE NORTH

In the far north are the mountain ranges and upland valleys of the Yukon and the Northwest Territories with their increasingly sparse vegetation. This was where the greatest gold rush in history took place in the late 19th century. The climatic contrasts here are as varied as the landscapes: damp, mild oceanic climate prevails on the Pacific coast, whereas the interior of Canada has a continental climate with hot summers and bitterly cold winters. High in the Arctic north, summer barely lasts for two months, while in the south – on the same latitude as the French wine region of Champagne – the Okanagan Valley in British Columbia is temperate enough for vineyards and peach orchards to thrive.

URBAN FLAIR, IN A FEW PLACES ONLY

Big cities are few and far between. Vancouver – surrounded by the sea – is considered one of the most beautiful cities on the North American continent. About 80 per cent of the population lives in the fertile valley of the Fraser River, in the temperate valleys around Kelowna and Kamloops and in Alberta's two metropolises. However, the mountain and Arctic areas are very sparsely populated. More than 10,000 years ago the ancestors of Native Americans settled in Western Canada. Their descendants maintain a significant presence in the region today and are increasingly confident in protecting their rights and cultural identity; this is especially evident along the west coast where totem poles and traditional plank houses can still be admired. Two hundred years ago, the first white explorers sailed along the west coast and began to trade fur with the First Nations; later in the 19th century, the first European settlers arrived: farmers from the Ukraine, England, Germany and Scandinavia.

WEALTH FROM THE LAND

Economically the West Canadians have remained true to the land: mining, ranching, fisheries and recently even wine, are the main industries in the southern provinces. Forestry is the mainstay in the relatively unexplored north. Still, there are huge, totally unspoilt and uninhabited landscapes offering plenty of space for wildlife enthusiasts.

AT A GLANCE

9.2 million
inhabitants in BC, Alberta, Yukon and NWT

United Kingdom: 68 million

60,000
PANCAKES
are baked on a single day for the Calgary Stampede

850m

length of the world's longest beaver dam in the Wood Buffalo National Park to the north of Alberta

3,233,000km²
combined area of BC, Alberta, Yukon and NWT

United Kingdom: 243,000km² (approx. 7.5%)

HIGHEST PEAK:
MOUNT LOGAN, YUKON
5,995m

Mont Blanc: 4,808m

−63°C
LOWEST TEMPERATURE EVER RECORDED IN CANADA (YUKON, 3 FEBRUARY 1947)

ANNUAL RAINFALL
ON MORESBY ISLAND
6,325mm

London: 690mm

14 NATIONAL PARKS IN WESTERN CANADA
Banff, Jasper, Waterton Lakes, Elk Island, Wood Buffalo, Kootenay, Yoho, Glacier, Mt. Revelstoke, Pacific Rim, Gwaii Haanas Kluane, Nahanni, Vuntut, Tuktut Nogait

VANCOUVER

Third largest Canadian city, 2.5 million inhabitants

25,700km
LENGTH OF THE PACIFIC COASTLINE including islands and fjords

HOH OHO
Canadian postcode for Father Christmas

UNDERSTAND CANADA WEST

THE HUNT FOR THE PUCK

During the winter, Saturday evening is always "Hockey Night" in Canada. The entire nation sits in front of the TV or in sports bars and cheers on the teams of the *National Hockey League (NHL)*. The US teams are also followed with great interest because many players in the American teams come from Canada.

The seamen who travelled with the English explorer John Franklin during the 19th century supposedly played hockey on the ice, thus initiating Canada's most popular sport. Western Canada's best teams are the *Vancouver Canucks*, *Calgary Flames* and *Edmonton Oilers*. Tickets for NHL games (Oct–April) are expensive and not always easy to come by. However, you can buy tickets on entry for games in the regional and college leagues, which are often just as exciting.

INSIDER TIP
Young hockey talent

FIRST NATIONS

The descendants of the original inhabitants of Canada are known as *First Nations*. With this term, Canadians recognise that the 617 tribes in the

Traditional gathering of the chiefs: the Blackfoot pow wow

country were living there long before white people arrived. The ancestors of the Native Americans probably came across the Bering Strait to North America 15,000–20,000 years ago. Over thousands of years they developed into independent cultural groups, with the semi-nomadic hunter tribes living in the north. The Plains tribes on the prairies of today's Alberta followed the vast herds of buffalo, while the Kwakiutl and Haida on the west coast became skilled woodcarvers. The ancestors of today's Inuit crossed the Canadian Arctic from Alaska about 1,000 years ago.

Today, there are around 700,000 Native American and 50,000 Inuit descendants of those "First Nations" in the country. Their rights as the original inhabitants of the continent were acknowledged with a section in the 1982 Constitution Act. This, and their growing self-confidence as indigenous people, led to numerous movements for land restitution and self-governance. The Inuit achieved the most spectacular success when, in 1999, they were given their own territory separate from the Northwest Territories, known as *Nunavut* (our land), which they govern and manage themselves.

FLORA & FAUNA

Most of Western Canada lies in the area of the boreal forest, which stretches like a broad band across the continent. These forests are the habitat of black and grizzly bears, moose, several deer species, lynxes, porcupines and beavers, and more recently the

TRUE OR FALSE?

ENGLISH CUSTOMS

Have you noticed that people in Canada tend to queue – at the check-in for a bear-watching tour, at the bus stop and the entrance to a restaurant? Basically everywhere, patiently and quite contently. There is no pushing and shoving. The British tradition is very much alive in post-colonial Canada.

WHAT CANADIANS EAT

It is a myth that maple syrup is served with all meals in Canada. And anyway, that wouldn't make sense in Western Canada because the syrup is harvested in the east of the country. The heavy lumberjack diet is another cliché. Of course, you can still find wonderful steaks on the menu, but the trend is moving towards sushi, vegan burgers, açai and poke.

FUR HATS ARE MANDATORY

It is always cold in Canada. And all Brits eat fish 'n' chips. Both are clichés. Vancouver is roughly at the same latitude as Paris and its climate is quite mild due to the nearby ocean. In summer it can get really hot in Western Canada, including the northern regions. However, if you visit in winter, you will definitely need to keep your fur hat on.

bark beetle – possibly a result of global warming – which is wreaking havoc in the interior of British Columbia.

The south and east of Alberta form part of the large North American prairie, originally a grass savannah, but due to its fertile soil the area is now mostly ploughed and covered by massive crop fields. What was once home to millions of bison is today the breadbasket of Canada – the bison remain in only a few protected areas. Alpine flora, with many wild flowers, flourishes in the Rocky Mountains, providing nourishment to mountain goats and sheep. On the western slopes of the Coast Mountains and on Vancouver Island are lush rain forests full of tall Douglas fir, Sitka spruce, red cedar and lush ferns.

To the north, the forests of taiga and tundra extend into the Yukon and the Northwest Territories. Only caribou, mountain hares and musk ox are able to live off the sparse lichens and mosses in this region. However, in the summer the large freshwater areas provide food for countless waterfowl.

PROTECTED FOR ALL ETERNITY

The forerunner of present-day Banff National Park was founded in 1885 "for the benefit, advantage and enjoyment of the people of Canada". It was the first in what is now a long list of parks, where the most beautiful and most pristine regions of the vast countryside are protected. The ecological aspects of the park system, mandated by the Canadian Ministry of the Environment, were considered to be groundbreaking.

The country's 47 national parks today cover a total of approximately 300,000km², with a further dozen parks being planned.

Approximately 30 million people visit the parks annually, and visitors must abide by park rules: no animals may be fed, no branch broken; picking a bunch of wild flowers can be an expensive experience – you may be fined up to C$500. Obviously, hunting is also prohibited, although you may fish in the streams and lakes provided you get a licence. For additional information please visit: *parkscanada.ca*.

THE QUEEN

Queen Elizabeth II is Canada's head of state because the nation is a parliamentary democracy within the British Commonwealth. The Queen does not have any power over the nation, but she performs occasional ceremonial tasks and either she or a member of her immediate family visits the country every ten years or so.

The federal capital is Ottawa, but Canada's ten provinces have extensive autonomy in matters of education, cultural policy, health care and use of natural resources. Only the three sparsely populated territories in the north are mostly financed and governed directly from Ottawa.

THE BIG SCREEN

If you look very closely, you can recognise the landscapes of the Rockies or Vancouver in various movies. Numerous Hollywood movies are actually filmed in Western Canada, with Vancouver being top of the list of filming locations. The Rockies provide a great backdrop for Westerns: Marilyn Monroe was filmed here in *River of No Return* and both *Brokeback Mountain* and the classic film *Little Big Man* were shot in the foothills of the mountains.

ENVIRONMENTAL PROTECTION

Despite the fact that the conservative government in Ottawa opted out of the Kyoto Protocol for climate protection in 2011, many Canadians see themselves as being environmentally conscious. Rubbish is separated and recycled, nature parks are created and environmental organisations are actively supported. Vancouver even aims to be the most environmentally friendly city in the world by creating cycle lanes and a commuter railway system.

While Western Canada is the birthplace of powerful environmental organisations – such as the *David Suzuki Foundation*, *Living Oceans Society* and *Greenpeace* – the country is still one of the world's largest squanderers. This is unsurprising because the Canadians have always had an abundant supply of mineral resources, energy and water, but they are now

Alberta is part of the "wheat belt", an area of arable land that stretches all the way to Texas

rethinking their ways. Learn more about environmental issues in Canada at *thegreenpages.ca*.

JUSTIN, THE CHARMER

The Prime Minister of Canada is young, for a world leader, and portrays himself as being in touch with the populace. He lists boxing as his hobby and was a high school teacher prior to his election. As the son of the former Prime Minister Pierre Trudeau, who enjoyed great popularity during the 1970s, his political talent is in his blood.

Since coming to power in 2015, he has brought more women and individuals from minority backgrounds into the cabinet. He is also known for viral videos and photos as can be seen on YouTube.

MOUNTIES

Dressed in red, the *Royal Canadian Mounted Police* are probably Canada's most famous and recognised symbol. In their parade uniform the *Mounties* perform at official events. However, they are much more than just a colourful accessory; today the highly trained federal police are responsible for all rural regions and jurisdictions in Canada that cannot afford their own police – and there are many in the sparsely populated west.

Founded in 1873, the RCMP force is today about 15,000 strong. For decades, the forts of the Mounties were also the only outposts of civilisation in the then rather wild west. The lawmen patrolled the Arctic with dog sleds, on horseback and by canoe, and

went into the most isolated gold mining camps. Even today you can experience the Mounties up close and personal – as armed guards on the highways who will fine you if you exceed the speed limit!

POP STARS? OH YES!

When Peter Fonda made the famous road trip movie *Easy Rider* the bikers cruised along on the open road to the legendary song "Born to be Wild". The soundtrack was by the band Steppenwolf and the members mostly came from Toronto. In fact many Canadian artists such as Leonard Cohen, Neil Young and Joni Mitchell moved down to the States, where Hollywood and the American music scene dominated. More recent Canadian singers include Bryan Adams, Céline Dion, Alanis Morissette, Avril Lavigne, Justin Bieber and Shania Twain.

WOODEN OSTENTATION

Adorned with elaborate, carved masks and mythical beasts, totem poles stand in front of government buildings and museums, while kitsch plastic replicas decorate the souvenir shops. Totem poles are the most recognisable symbol of Native American culture.

Originally, this highly developed wood-carving art was only part of the culture of the Northwest Coast Native Americans – the area between Vancouver Island and the southeast of Alaska. Totem poles were not religious icons but symbols of prestige, power and wealth for a clan or a chief. For

Today, Mounties in their red uniform are mostly seen at official ceremonies

decades the "pagan carvings" were banned by the state and missionaries, but this ancient art form is undergoing a revival. Beautiful totem poles are on display in the museums of Vancouver and Victoria, or you can drive to the First Nation villages up the west coast to see many original totem poles that have been preserved in Alert Bay, Quadra Island and Hazelton, among others.

GOLD

The publication of Jack London's novels spread the story of the Klondike gold rush. The search for gold played a very special role in Canadian history, because its discovery opened up the whole western region.

Around 1860, the gold rush in the Cariboo Mountains attracted thousands of miners. Thirty years later the call of "Gold in the Yukon!" resulted in 100,000 prospectors toiling laboriously through ice and snow in the Coast Mountains to reach the promised land in time for spring. In just three years gold worth 100 million dollars was found, and Dawson City became the largest city west of Winnipeg, with 30,000 inhabitants.

Gold is still being mined to this day – in Klondike, in Yellowknife and in the hard granite rock of the Canadian Shield in Eastern Canada. Some four million ounces are mined annually, of which a large part goes to producing the *Maple Leaf Dollar*, one of the best-selling gold coins in the world.

EATING
SHOPPING
SPORT

Baker Street in Nelson

EATING & DRINKING

There is no Canadian national dish: the country is simply too big. Immigrant groups have come from all over the world, adding multicultural diversity and culinary variety to Western Canada's cuisine.

In all the major cities, you will be able to enjoy excellent Chinese, Indian and Italian restaurants. The fresh fish from the Pacific is of the highest quality, making sushi another popular choice. Aside from fresh salmon (in many varieties) there is, of course, Canada's famous grilled steak, often served with baked potatoes and corn on the cob.

FAST OR REGIONAL?

You will be confronted with the usual monotony of hamburgers and grilled chicken. There are fast-food restaurants serving breakfast and lunch everywhere in Canada. But if you look beyond the flashing neon signs you will find smaller venues offering good home-cooked meals – the small fish restaurants on Vancouver Island, rustic lodges in the wilderness or international restaurants in the cities. In Alberta, meat eaters should try a steak – either in a restaurant or barbecued on your own campfire. The cattle roam wild on huge ranches, the meat is unsurpassable and the portions are designed for hungry lumberjacks. West of the Rocky Mountains, seafood is the main culinary attraction: it's deliciously fresh on Vancouver Island and along the Sunshine Coast north of Vancouver. Poached or grilled salmon (*sockeye salmon* is best) with fresh vegetables from Fraser Valley and a crisp white wine from sunny Okanagan Valley is among the finest Canada has to offer. There is also a growing trend towards vegan and vegetarian diets.

Oysters and lobster (left), Tim Hortons coffee shop (right)

GOURMET FOOD

In the style of the new California cuisine that emerged in the 1970s in San Francisco and Los Angeles, Vancouver and Victoria have developed a west coast style. The methods of preparation and the spices used come from all over the world. The produce, however, is locally grown and ecologically sound: vegetables from the Fraser Valley, peaches, apples and grapes from the Okanagan Valley, crab, halibut and salmon straight from the Pacific. The talented young chefs understand how to harmonize the flavours and how to bring out the different tastes. Sometimes, they use traditional Native American cooking methods, such as grilling the salmon on planks of cedar. And for dessert it's ice cream with wild berries.

WHAT TO EAT AND WHEN?

Your best bet for breakfast is in a coffee shop. You can order either a small continental breakfast (juice, coffee, toast and marmalade) or a large American breakfast with bacon and eggs. For lunch Canadians often eat smaller meals – a simple salad or soup and sandwich. In the rural regions, dinner is often served early, between 5.30pm and 7pm; in the larger cities between 7pm and 9pm.

Be aware that the final amount of the bill may be more than you anticipated, as prices shown on the menu do not include *tax* (which differs from province to province). The tip is not usually included so, if you are happy with the service, then a 15–20 per cent tip is the norm.

QUALITY MADE IN CANADA

Earls and the *Cactus Club*, popular local chains in the greater Vancouver area, offer excellent dishes ranging from pasta to steaks and omelettes in the morning. *The Keg* chain is famous for good (but not exactly cheap) steaks, while *Triple O White Spot* is a good choice if you long for a decent burger or freshly baked doughnut at a reasonable price. Many Canadians pop into a *Tim Hortons* for good coffee and a fresh doughnut. The chain also serves affordable soups and sandwiches and is more popular than Starbucks.

TO QUENCH A LUMBERJACK'S THIRST

If there is a national drink in Canada, then it is the aromatic and very palatable beer, which goes well with a hearty steak. Everywhere in the country you will find *Molson Canadian* or *Labatt's Blue*, while speciality beers, such as *Kokanee*, are served only in some regions. Microbreweries have become increasingly popular in recent years. In British Columbia you should try the beers by *Okanagan Spring* and *Granville Island*, while in Alberta beers by the *Wild Rose Brewing Company* from Calgary or by *Jasper Brewing* are worth sampling.

Despite most wines being imported from California, the local wines from the Okanagan Valley are definitely worth tasting – the ice wine is excellent. If you want something stronger, go for the excellent Canadian whiskey. A speciality of the north is *Yukon Jack*, a devastatingly strong whiskey liqueur ideal for the long, cold winter nights.

INSIDER TIP
Whiskey liqueur for the winter

In addition to the usual hotel bars there are also many rustic bars with a pool table and a long bar counter – often the best place to meet the locals. And in West Canada, a cabaret is a bar with country and western bands performing most weekends.

Delicious wine from the Okanagan Valley

Today's Specials

Breakfast

BC BENNY
Bread roll with poached eggs, smoked salmon and hollandaise sauce on a roll

FRENCH TOAST WITH FRESH BERRIES

PANCAKES WITH MAPLE SYRUP

Starters

CLAM/SEAFOOD CHOWDER
Hearty cream-based mussel or fish soup

BUFFALO WINGS
Chicken wings, marinated in a spicy sauce, then fried or grilled

Main courses

POACHED SOCKEYE SALMON
Freshly caught red salmon

DUNGENESS CRAB
A large species of crab found along the west coast

PRIME RIB (STEAK)
Very tender beef from the prime rib

Desserts

BEAVERTAIL
Fried pastry sprinkled with cinnamon and sugar

BUTTER TART
Pastry tart with a butter, syrup and sugar filling

Drinks

CAESAR
Spicy drink made of vodka with tomato and mussel juice

WEST COAST IPA
A slightly bitter, hoppy lager from the Granville Island Brewery

ICE WINE
Sweet wine produced from grapes that are left on the vine in sub-zero temperatures

SHOPPING

Western Canada is not necessarily known as a shopping destination. In the cities there is an excellent variety of shops; elsewhere, your options decrease dramatically. A general store – a small grocery store that also sells everything including shoes and chainsaws – has to suffice in the small towns. The further north you go, the more expensive everything becomes.

Regional products such as wild flower honey from the prairies or marmalade and wine from the Okanagan Valley are popular souvenirs. The most delicious salmon, called *Indian Candy*, has been candied and smoked.

INSIDER TIP
Salmon Indian style

The most famous Canadian souvenir is maple syrup. The thickened sap from maple trees is an essential part of a hearty pancake breakfast in Canada.

NATIVE AMERICAN ART

Native American and Inuit arts and crafts are not cheap, the best option is to buy directly in the reservations, in reputable galleries or in the shops of the major museums. The west coast tribes, once famous for their totem poles, today carve smaller objects such as masks or bowls and also use the stylised animal symbols in their silver jewellery and drawings.

Native Americans in the northern regions traditionally make moose-leather moccasins, as well as woven baskets and beaded leather jackets. The Inuit of the Arctic are famous for their beautiful soapstone sculptures. Be aware that the import of whale-bone sculptures is prohibited.

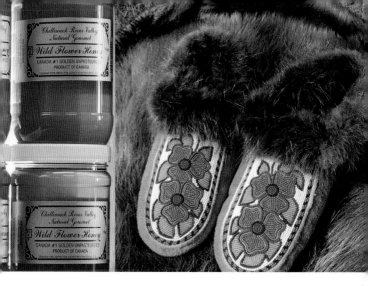

Honey from British Columbia (left) and moose-hide moccasins (right)

CHEAP & TRENDY

Casual wear and sports gear are cheaper here than in Europe. Outlet shopping is still widely unknown in Western Canada, with the exception of a few malls in the region between Calgary and Edmonton. The Canadian chain 🐖 *Winners* specialises in discount sales of old stock, cheap jeans and children's clothing. Canadian sportswear brands such as *Lululemon Athletica* and *Roots Canada*, whose designers also dress the Canadian Olympic squad, are very popular with the fashion-conscious youth, but are more expensive.

MOSQUITO-PROOF FASHION

Chequered lumberjack shirts became fashionable around 100 years ago and haven't changed much since. However, they are practical. The fabric has to be thick and the fit loose in order to prevent mosquito bites. You can buy them in shops such as the 🐖 *Mark's Work Wearhouse* chain.

REGIONAL GIFTS

In the coastal villages of Vancouver Island and in Vancouver, you will find the beautiful, chunky Cowichan sweaters and handicrafts made of wood, clay and ceramic. Many artists, who exhibit in the galleries of Victoria, live on the Gulf Islands off Vancouver Island. Ideal souvenirs from Alberta are top-quality Stetson hats, silver belt buckles and handmade (or even custom-made) boots.

SPORT & ACTIVITIES

Whether hiking, canoeing or riding, the rugged coastline of the Pacific Ocean and peaks of the Rockies both provide amazing backdrops.

Thanks to the pioneers, the outdoor lifestyle is a way of life for Canadians, and active holidays are made easy for visitors because hiking and cycling trails are to be found everywhere.

Every major hotel and holiday resort has their own fitness centre and often a golf course. Numerous *rental shops* rent out canoes, bicycles and other sporting equipment – and can provide tips and maps. Organised day tours can also be booked at short notice. However, longer excursions are best booked in advance.

CANOE, KAYAK & RUBBER DINGHY

The canoe was invented in Canada and, while they used to be made of tree bark, up-to-date models are aluminium-based. You can rent them in many lodges and from various outfitters. Sea kayaking tours in the west coast island labyrinth and rubber dinghy trips are also popular.

Majestic Ocean Kayaking offer day trips in kayaks and a great selection of multi-day tours around the islands of the west coast in the Pacific Rim National Park. *1167 Helen Rd | Ucluelet | tel. 250 7 26 28 68 | oceankayaking.com*

Sunwolf offer full-day rubber dinghy trips on the Elaho River near Whistler. For families, half-day and more gentle floating trips are available. *70002 Squamish Valley Rd | Brackendale | tel. 604 8 98 15 37 | sunwolf.net*

Timberwolf Tours offer multi-day guided canoe trips and adventure tours in the Rockies. *Site 34, 51404 RR264 | Spruce Grove | Alberta | tel. 780 4 70 49 66 | timberwolftours.com*

Winter fun in Whistler

CYCLING

Bicycles for day trips *(around C$20–40 per day, C$70–150 per week)* are readily available in the towns of the south. For longer rides, the Gulf Islands off Vancouver and the Okanagan Valley are ideal as are the old railway tracks in the Kettle Valley and the Rockies – here, however, you do need to be quite fit. For mountain bike enthusiasts there is the annual *Trans-Rockies Bike Race* (transrockies.com).

In summer, *Soul Ski & Bike* provide bike rentals as well as day tours and multi-day tours in Banff National Park and on the Icefields Parkway. *203 A Bear St | Banff | tel. 403 7 60 16 50 | banffsoul.com*

Whistler Mountain Bike Park is the ultimate playground for mountain bikers: summer lifts and a 1,200m difference in altitude; mid-July *Bike Festival | tel. 800 7 66 04 49 | bike. whistlerblackcomb.com*

FISHING

Most anglers dream about Pacific salmon, but the fun is not cheap: from C$50 for a guided day trip and C$10,000 or more for a week in an exclusive fishing resort. Amateur anglers may fish anywhere as long as they have a licence (C$20–100 depending on the permit period), which is available from sports stores and lodges.

April Point Lodge is a dream location for salmon fishermen surrounded, as it is, by rocks, waves and woods near Campbell River and well-stocked with fish, in the archipelago near Vancouver Island. *Quadra Island | tel. 250 2 86 11 02 | aprilpoint.com*

Englefield Bay and *Hippa Island* are good spots for hard-core salmon fishermen and women: two floating lodges of the Haida tribe, located far away from civilisation in the coves of Haida Gwaii. *Tel. 800 8 10 89 33 | westcoastresorts.com*

GOLF

Golf is a national sport in Canada and there are many courses. The greens are mostly open to the public. Also non-club members without a handicap are welcome and green fees are affordable *(C$50–100)*. The most beautiful and expensive courses are in the Rockies, such as the legendary Fairmont Courses in Banff or Jasper National Park and those in Invermere or Kananaskis. For details, please visit *albertagolf.org, golftherockies.net and britishcolumbiagolf.org.*

HIKING

The largest selection of trails – signposted and well maintained – are in the national and provincial parks. Wardens in the visitor centres are helpful and provide information about the best trails. Good track networks exist, for example, in Banff, Yoho and Jasper national parks. Hiking outside of the parks is often difficult – in Canada, wilderness really does mean wilderness.

HORSE RIDING

Anyone can enjoy an hour or two of trail riding. You don't need to be experienced as they use Western-style saddles and the horses walk very obediently in a row. Rides can be booked

at many ranches at short notice. Experienced riders can book ranch holidays and ride with the cowboys all day long. Please visit *bcguestranches. com* and *thecowboytrail.com*.

Rangeview Ranch is a rustic *working ranch* in the foothills of the Rockies near Waterton Lakes Park. *Box 28, Site 10 | Cardston | tel. 403 6 53 28 21 | rangeviewranch.com*

Ten-ee-ah Lodge is a well-maintained log cabin lodge with a riding program and other activities in British Columbia. There is also a campsite. *Lac La Hache | tel. 250 4 34 97 45 | ten-ee-ah.bc.ca*

All major national parks offer hiking trails for all levels of difficulty

ROPE COURSES & ZIP LINES

Adrenaline rush: in recent years, rope and adventure courses for adults (and children) have been popping up throughout Canada. Zip lining through canyons and over streams or above the forest has become a popular activity. There are also rock-climbing centres where you brave an obstacle course, often made more difficult with jumps from heights. All the guides are trained and the equipment is safe and well secured – guaranteed fun. For more information, please visit *ziplinerider.com* and *wildplay.com*.

WINTER SPORTS

The powder snow in the Rocky Mountains is legendary. Ski areas such as Banff, Lake Louise, Fernie or Big White offer excellent ski slopes. The largest winter sports area is Whistler, the Olympic venue on the west coast.

Experienced skiers can also enjoy the – admittedly not very environmentally friendly – thrill of heli-skiing in central British Columbia.

REGIONAL OVERVIEW

BEAUFORT SEA

USA

Great Bear Lake

Whitehorse ✈

BRITISH COLUMBIA p. 64

Classic Canada: forests, mountains and lakes →

PACIFIC OCEAN

Prince George

Hike on the wild beaches of the Pacific

VANCOUVER ISLAND p. 50

Kamloops

Vancouver ✈

Kelowna

Victoria

USA

200 km
124.3 mi

Celebrate in Canada's most beautiful city and enjoy fresh sushi

VANCOUVER p. 38

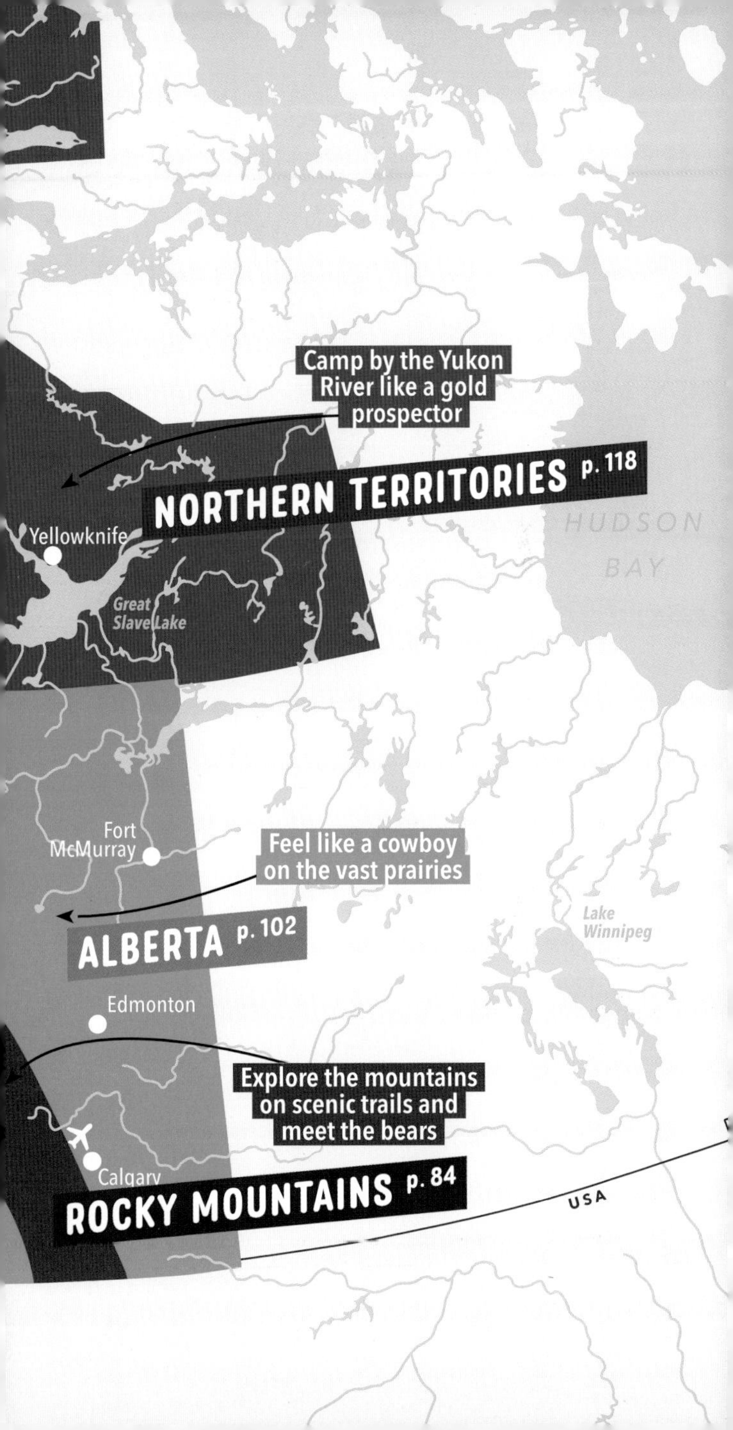

Camp by the Yukon River like a gold prospector

NORTHERN TERRITORIES p. 118

HUDSON BAY

Yellowknife

Great Slave Lake

Fort McMurray

Feel like a cowboy on the vast prairies

ALBERTA p. 102

Lake Winnipeg

Edmonton

Explore the mountains on scenic trails and meet the bears

Calgary

ROCKY MOUNTAINS p. 84

USA

VANCOUVER

THE JEWEL OF THE WEST COAST

Vancouver is a young, vibrant city with a captivating charm and casual, European flair; a dynamic metropolis set against a dramatic backdrop of dark green mountains in the broad delta of the Fraser River. Its restored Victorian homes, spacious parks and beaches are surrounded by plenty of unspoilt nature.

With approximately 2.5 million inhabitants (in the greater metropolitan area of the Fraser Delta), Vancouver is today the most important economic and commercial centre on the Pacific coast.

The view from Stanley Park to the marina

Three universities, numerous museums and theatres make it the cultural hub of the region. In recent years, so many films have been shot in the city that it now has the nickname of "Hollywood North". When Captain George Vancouver discovered the mouth of the Fraser River in 1792, there were only huge Douglas fir forests. In 1886, when Vancouver became the terminal station of the transcontinental railway, it started to grow, eventually becoming a metropolis which even hosted the Olympic Winter Games in 2010.

VANCOUVER

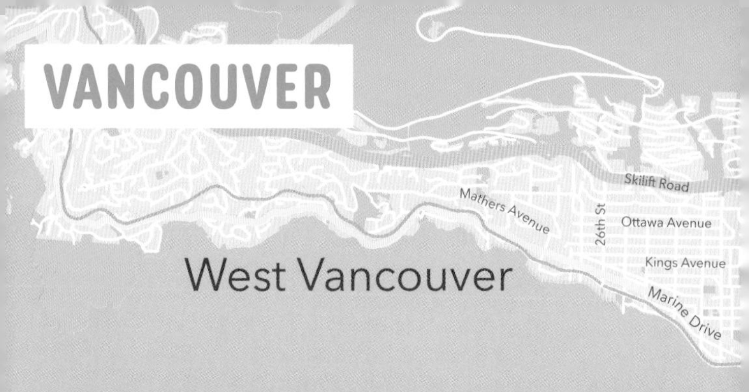

West Vancouver

West Vancouver

MARCO POLO HIGHLIGHTS

★ **CANADA PLACE**
The promenade at the cruise liner pier with cafés and magnificent views ➤ p. 42

★ **STANLEY PARK**
Canada's most beautiful urban park – ideal for a bike ride ➤ p. 42

★ **GASTOWN**
Souvenirs and a hooting steam clock: the rather nice tourist strip ➤ p. 43

★ **UBC MUSEUM OF ANTHROPOLOGY**
Genuine totem poles and masks of the north-west coast First Nations ➤ p. 45

★ **GRANVILLE ISLAND PUBLIC MARKET**
Salmon, steaks, delicious pies, fresh raspberries – Canada's full range of offerings ➤ p. 46

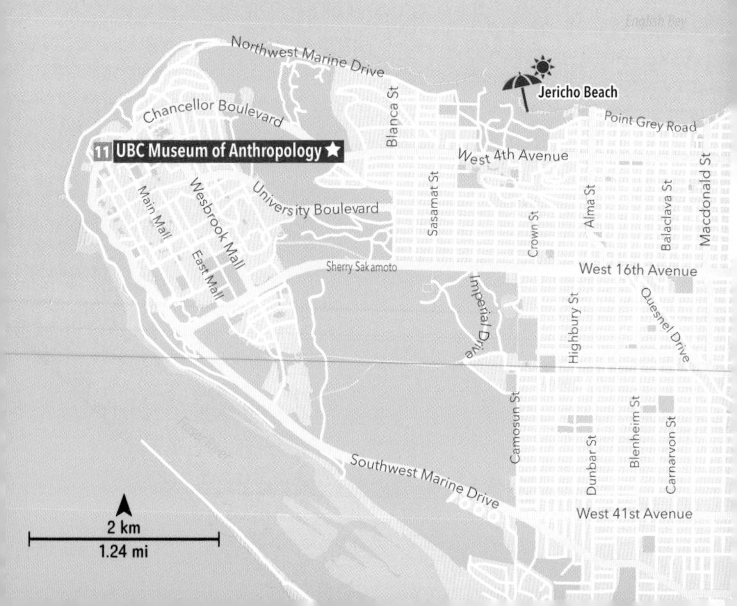

Northwest Marine Drive

English Bay

Jericho Beach

Point Grey Road

Chancellor Boulevard

Blanca St

11 **UBC Museum of Anthropology ★**

West 4th Avenue

Sasamat St

Crown St

Alma St

Balaclava St

Macdonald St

Main Mall

Wesbrook Mall

University Boulevard

East Mall

Sherry Sakamoto

West 16th Avenue

Imperial Drive

Highbury St

Quesnel Drive

Camosun St

Dunbar St

Blenheim St

Carnarvon St

Southwest Marine Drive

West 41st Avenue

▲
2 km
1.24 mi

Millstream Road

14 Capilano Salmon Hatchery

Southborough Drive

Stevens Drive

Dreamweaver

Baden Powell Trail

Capilano Suspension Bridge 13

Edgemont Boulevard

Highland Boulevard

Delbrook Avenue

Road

West Queens Road

East 29th St

Kings Avenue

nglewood Avenue

West 25th St

Taylor Way

Keith Road

Larson Road

Mahon Avenue

Lonsdale Avenue

Grand Boulevard East

Esquimalt Avenue

Capilano

🛍 **Lululemon**

Marine Drive

Fell Avenue

Welch Street

Pemberton Avenue

West 1st Street

West 3rd St

East Keith Road

Lions Gate Bridge

🛍 **Lonsdale Quay Market**

Low Level Road

Stanley Park Causeway

North Vancouver

Pipeline Road

Vancouver Harbour

3 Stanley Park ★

🍴 **Lift**

Kingyo 🍴 🍴 **Dinesty**

🍴 **Tapshack**

1 Canada Place ★

English Bay Beach ☀

🍴 **Caffe Artigiano**

Stewart St

Dundas St

Bill Reid Gallery 2

4 Gastown ★

East Hastings St

Kitsilano Beach ☀

Davie St

Seymour St

5 Chinatown

9 Maritime Museum

Prior St

Venables St

10 Vancouver Museum

7 Yaletown

Vancouver Farmers Market

🚆

The Sandbar

Science World 6

🍴 **Marcello Pizzeria**

🍴 **Cacao**

8 Granville Island

East 1st Avenue

Edible Canada

Commercial Drive

Rain or Shine

🛍 **MEC (Mountain Equipment Co-op)**

Granville Island Public Market ★

West Broadway

East Broadway

East 12th Avenue

Cambie St

Main St

Kingsway

Nanaimo Street

Arbutus St

West King Edward Avenue

Granville Street

Oak St

East King Edward Avenue

Vancouver

Fraser St

Knight St

Victoria Drive

12 Van Dusen Botanical Garden

West 41st Avenue

East 41st Avenue

VANCOUVER

SIGHTSEEING

You can get a good initial overview of the city from the *The Lookout* terrace in the Harbour Centre (*e3*) on Hastings Street or – even better – a gondola ride on the aerial tramway system up *Grouse Mountain* with spectacular views of the city. Back on the ground, explore the city on foot or by rental bicycle. *Vancouver Trolleys (daily 9am–6pm | fare C$34–54)* offers two guided bus tours along fixed routes that cover all city attractions. Buses run every 20 minutes and you can hop on and off as you wish. Tourist information: *200 Burrard St | tourism vancouver.com*

■ CANADA PLACE ★

During Expo 86 the pier, with its snow-white tent design by architect Ed Zeidler, was the Canada Pavilion. It's perfect for a stroll to watch cruise ships coming and going and to enjoy the view over the fjord from the top of the pier *(Cordova St/Howe St)*. The *Vancouver Convention Centre* next door was constructed in 2010 with sustainable technologies, demonstrating Vancouver's aim to be Canada's "greenest" city: it served as the gigantic hall of the International Media Centre for the Olympic Winter Games. *e3*

■ BILL REID GALLERY

Not particularly big, but very interesting: works of the famous Native American artist who died in 1998. *Daily 10am–5pm, winter closed Mon/Tue | admission C$13 | 639 Hornby St |* ○ *1 hr | d3*

■ STANLEY PARK ★

A beautiful urban park with hiking trails and picnic areas where there are some original totem poles surrounded by a dense forest of ancient Douglas firs. Built in 1938, the *Lions Gate Bridge* at the northern tip of the park connects the city to North Vancouver. You can cycle around the peninsula, on which the park is situated, on the 10-km-long ▶ *Stanley Park Drive (bicycle rental near the Denman St entrance | C$25–50 for half a day)*. The 1,000-acre park also incorporates the ⚐ *Vancouver Aquarium* with dolphins, fur seals, sea otters and an exhibition on the migration of salmon *(daily in summer 9.30am–6pm, otherwise 10am–5pm | admission C$38)*.

WHERE TO START?

Start at central **Robson Square** (*c–d4)*. The Robson Street shopping district starts toward the west and further north is the old town around Water Street, Canada Place and the Seawall waterfront promenade at the Burrard Inlet. Within walking distance are Yaletown and the beaches in the West End, close to Denman Street and Stanley Park. You can park in the Pacific Centre Mall at Robson/Granville Street. The closest Skytrain Stations are Granville and City Centre.

Have you seen the smoke? A steam clock tells the time in the historic Gastown quarter

Children can enjoy a 👯 *narrow-gauge railway*, a heated salt-water pool on *Second Beach* and a water park with gushing fountains at *Lumberman's Arch*. ▢ *a–d1*

4 GASTOWN ★

This district, whose boundary runs along Water Streeet, is the restored old town of Vancouver. Today, the old brick buildings house shops, restaurants and art galleries. A fun attraction is the *Steam Clock* on the corner of Cambie Street which is powered by steam from the municipal heating grid. A statue of city founder John "Gassy Jack" Deighton is just east at the Water/Carr Street intersection. It is assumed that he was the one who built the first house in Vancouver in 1867: a saloon. This established a tradition and today there are still numerous pubs around the square. ▢ *e4*

5 CHINATOWN

Around Pender and Main Street is the busy and somewhat grubby old Chinatown of Vancouver, which has become trendy again in recent years with hot spots and clubs. Worth seeing is the *Dr Sun Yat-Sen Classical Chinese Garden* on Carrall Street. On Friday to Sunday evenings there is the *Night Market* around Main/Keefer Street with many stalls. Also well worth a visit is the modern *T&T Supermarket (Keefer St/Abbott St)* which offers every imaginable Asian product, including fish and exotic fruit. ▢ *f4*

INSIDER TIP
Exotic products for sale

6 SCIENCE WORLD 👯

The glass ball of the Expo 86 at False Creek is now a museum of technology for children, containing many hands-on experiments as well as a

360-degree cinema. *Mon–Fri 10am–5pm, Sat/Sun 10am–6pm | admission C$25, children C$ 17 | 1455 Quebec St | scienceworld.ca | ⏱ 2 hrs | 🔲 e–f5*

7 YALETOWN

The city's trendy district: during the day it's the quirky boutiques along Hamilton and Mainland Street that attract visitors, and at night it is the chic restaurants, brew pubs and bars. 🔲 *d5*

8 GRANVILLE ISLAND

The restored waterfront harbour area underneath Granville Bridge is another attractive area in Vancouver: do some shopping at the famous 🚩 *Public Market*, browse colourful art shops like the *Gallery of BC Ceramics (1359 Cartwright St)* or eat ice cream with a view of houseboats and the city skyline. Not to be missed: *Railspur Alley* with artist studios and innovative galleries. There is even a 🧸 *Kids Market (2699 Granville St)*, a two-storey warehouse full of toys, sweets and soft toys. 🔲 *b–c6*

9 MARITIME MUSEUM

The crown in the museum's jewel is the *St Roch*, an Arctic patrol ship. The wooden schooner traversed the Northwest Passage several times. *Daily 10am–5pm, Thu until 8pm | admission C$13.50 | 1905 Ogden Av. | ⏱ 1 hr | 🔲 a5*

UBC Museum of Anthropology: Bill Reid took inspiration from ancestral legends

🔟 VANCOUVER MUSEUM

The large Rotunda on the shore of English Bay houses exhibits on the history of the city of Vancouver, the natural history of the area as well as Native American craftwork. Adjacent is the *MacMillan Space Centre & Planetarium*, with evening laser shows. *Daily 10am–5pm, Thu until 8pm, Fri/Sat until 9pm | admission C$19 | 1100 Chestnut St | 🕐 2 hrs | ⌗ a5*

1️⃣1️⃣ UBC MUSEUM OF ANTHROPOLOGY ★

Arthur Erickson's unconventional museum building in the grounds of the University of British Columbia houses an important collection of totem poles and masks of the Northwest Coast First Nations. There are beautiful historic carvings from Argyllit as well as modern works by Bill Reid. *Daily in summer 10am–5pm, Thu 10am–9pm, Oct–mid-May closed Mon | admission C$18 | 6393 NW Marine Dr. | 🕐 2 hrs | ⌗ F14*

1️⃣2️⃣ VANDUSEN BOTANICAL GARDEN

The garden covers 55 acres and is full of plants, flowers, groves, idyllic paths and small lakes. It is particularly colourful from May to July. *Daily 9am–8pm; winter 10am–3pm | admission C$11.25 | 5251 Oak St | ⌗ F14*

1️⃣3️⃣ CAPILANO SUSPENSION BRIDGE

A swaying, almost 140m-long suspension bridge spans the 70m-deep canyon. There is also a totem pole park, as well as a spectacular *cliff walk* high above the gorge and a giant souvenir shop. However, this tourist attraction can get crowded. *Daily in summer 8.30am–8pm, otherwise 9am–5pm | admission C$47 | North Vancouver | ⌗ F14*

1️⃣4️⃣ CAPILANO SALMON HATCHERY 🐟

Here you can view the life cycle of salmon through underwater gallery windows and information panels. From mid-August, the adult salmon return. *Daily in summer 8am–8pm | admission free | North Vancouver | Capilano Rd | ⌗ F14*

EATING & DRINKING

CACAO

INSIDER TIP
South America meets Canada

The Venezuelan chef Jefferson Alvarez creates food worthy of stars in his kitchen: octopus with pineapple salsa and delicious yucca chips. Booking required. *1898 W 1st Av. | tel. 604 7 31 53 70 | cacaovancouver.com | C$$–$$$ | ⌗ a6*

CAFFE ARTIGIANO

Popular café chain with excellent cappuccino, breakfast and snacks; there are branches at *1101 W Pender St and 740 W Hastings St | C$ | ⌗ d3*

DINESTY

Modern Chinese restaurant in the young West end of the inner city; excellent *Shanghai dumplings. 1719 Robson St | tel. 604 6 69 77 69 | C$$ | ⌗ b2*

EDIBLE CANADA
Trendy organic bistro with terrace and shop. Delicious *fish tacos* from their street stall, and if you arrive in an electric car, there is a charging station right outside the door. *1596 Johnston St | Granville Island | tel. 604 6 82 66 81 | ediblecanada.com | C$$ | ▢ b5*

GRANVILLE ISLAND PUBLIC MARKET ★ ▸
A display of Vancouver's culinary variety: mountains of fruit and berries, fresh bagels, steaks and smoked salmon. There are also stalls offering snacks from sushi to gyros as well as local arts and crafts. *Daily 9am–7pm | Granville Island | ▢ b5*

KINGYO
Japanese restaurant popular with the young Asian set, serving amazing creations. *871 Denman St | tel. 604 6 08 16 77 | kingyo-izakaya.ca | C$$ | ▢ b2*

LIFT
A nice bistro with a large waterside terrace and wonderful views of Stanley Park, mountains and water. *333 Menchion Mews | tel. 604 6 89 54 38 | liftbarandgrill.com | C$$–$$$ | ▢ c2*

MARCELLO PIZZERIA
Great pizza, cosy restaurant with a terrace in a funky bohemian quarter in the eastern part of the city. It's surrounded by numerous coffee shops and unconventional small retail shops. *1404 Commercial Dr. | Granville Island | tel. 604 2 15 77 60 | C$$ | ▢ f1*

RAIN OR SHINE
For ice cream lovers. You just have to try "nuts with Bourbon whiskey". Excellent location in the Kitsilano student quarter. *1926 W 4th Av. | rainorshineicecream.com | C$ | ▢ a6*

THE SANDBAR

INSIDER TIP
Dining under the bridge

Excellent fish served in all kinds of ways, large bar and heated rooftop terrace with fireplace, above False Creek. *1535 Johnston St | Granville Island | tel. 604 6 69 90 30 | C$$ | ▢ c6*

CANADIAN INNOVATIONS

The telephone, matches and the zipper – did you know that they all come from Canada? And the Canadians have invented a whole lot more, such as the snowmobile and the combine harvester. In 1879, the enormous size of Western Canada led the railway engineer Sanford Fleming to divide the earth into 24 time zones. Canada has also contributed with medical innovations: in 1929, Frederick Banting and John James Rickard Macleod developed the diabetes drug insulin, and in 1951 the engineer John Hopps developed the first pacemaker. Today, Canadian researchers are at the forefront of AIDS and genetic research.

A paradise of fresh produce in great variety: Granville Island Public Market

TAPSHACK
Ideal for a break on the promenade at Coal Harbour. *1199 W Cordova St | tel. 604 6 87 64 55 | C$–$$ |* ▥ *c2*

SHOPPING

The main shopping street is the lively *Robson Street. The Bay* department store and the large *Pacific Centre* mall are to the north of Robson Square.

LONSDALE QUAY MARKET 🐷
You can get to this market with its many stalls and original retail shops by the ferry pier in North Vancouver with the small *SeaBus* ferries *(ticket C$4.20)* in approx. 15 minutes. Beautiful views of the city. ▥ *f1*

LULULEMON
En vogue yoga clothing for beautiful bodies. In the large and exquisite Park Royal shopping centre directly on the northern side of the Lions Gate Bridge. *1000 Main St | West Vancouver | lululemon.com.* ▥ *e1*

MEC (MOUNTAIN EQUIPMENT CO-OP)
The mother of all outdoor shops, offering everything you need for all kinds of sports. *130 W Broadway | mec.ca |* ▥ *F14*

VANCOUVER FARMERS MARKET
In summer, farmers' markets are held in several city quarters, featuring food stalls, music and many different organic products. For details please visit: *eatlocal.org*

SPORT & ACTIVITIES

ECOMARINE PADDLING CENTRE

Rent kayaks and SUP (stand-up paddle) boards here for customised tours on False Creek with a city centre backdrop. Courses and guided tours. Rental: C$30–59 for 2 hours. *1668 Duranleau St | Granville Island | tel. 604 6 89 75 75 | ecomarine.com | ▢ b5*

NIGHTLIFE

Listings for current concerts and clubs are in the weekly publication *Georgia Straight*, the monthly magazine *Where Vancouver*, and in the weekend edition of the *Vancouver Sun*. Tickets for concerts, theatre shows and sporting events are available at ☛ *Tickets Tonight* in the *Vancouver Tourist Info*

English Bay Beach: Vancouver's most popular beach is close to the city centre

BEACHES

Though the waters of the Pacific Ocean are relatively chilly even in summer, the beaches of *English Bay* are nice for a quick dip and some sunbathing, even at the bottom of Denman Street. *Kitsilano Beach* (beach volleyball) and *Jericho Beach* located southwest of the city centre are best.

Centre (*Waterfront Centre | 200 Burrard St | ticketstonight.ca*). Downtown (▢ d4) nightlife focuses on Gastown – where there are good pubs such as the *Portside Pub (7 Alexander St)* or the *Charles Bar (136 Cordova St)* – in the WestEnd around *Davie* and *Denman St*, and in *Yaletown* (▢ d5), where you'll find the popular brew pub *Yaletown Brewing Co. (1111*

Mainland St, with restaurant). At weekends, the young queue up in front of the many clubs on *Granville Street* (▨ d4) and meet in the *Commodore Ballroom* to enjoy reggae, deep house and funk *(868 Granville St).*

AROUND VANCOUVER

LANGLEY
50km / 50 mins by car from Vancouver
Fort Langley National Historic Site (daily 9am–5pm | admission C$7.80),* the old fur-trading fort on the Fraser River and on Hwy 1, is today a museum village. The "inhabitants" of the old trading post guide you through the harsh lifestyle of the trappers in the 19th century. Fort Langley town itself also deserves a stroll. The picturesque main street, Glover Road, is lined with shady trees, numerous antique shops, boutiques and pleasant restaurants, such as the *Blacksmith Bakery (9190 Church St | C$$) selling superb chocolate croissants. ▨ F14

INSIDER TIP
Sustenance while strolling

RICHMOND
15km / 30 mins by Canada Line metro rail from Vancouver
Vancouver's Chinese neighbourhood is to the south of the city centre, not far from the airport. *No. 3 Road* features Asian shopping malls and numerous restaurants. Try the excellent dim sum for lunch at the elegant *Shanghai River* restaurant *(7831 Westminster Hwy. | tel. 604 2 33 88 85 | C$$).* Nearby, on the banks of the Fraser River, is the distinctive *Richmond Oval,* venue of the Olympic speed skating events.

On Richmond's south side is the old fishing harbour of *Steveston,* a lovely location for strolling along the harbour pier. It remains the base of Vancouver's fishing fleet, and the old can factory *Gulf of Georgia Cannery (12138 4th Av.),* which is now a museum, tells you the history of salmon fishing on the west coast. ▨ F14

WHERE TO STAY IN VANCOUVER

PURE LUXURY
If you are looking for something sumptuous, you are guaranteed a good night's sleep in the *Fairmont Waterfront (489 rooms | 900 Canada Place Way | tel. 604 6 91 19 91 | fairmont.com | C$$$ | ▨ d3),* a luxurious hotel in a prime location between the harbour promenade and Gastown. The ocean-facing rooms have full-height windows, offering beautiful views of the Burrard Inlet.

A HOTEL WITH CHARACTER
The *Sylvia,* a 1912 ivy-covered hotel in the West End, is simply charming and is located right on English Bay beach *(119 rooms | 1154 Gilford St. | tel. 604 6 81 93 21 | sylviahotel. com | C$–$$ | ▨ a3).*

VANCOUVER ISLAND

FROM MILD TO WILD

Whales, bears, rainforest, fjords, 2,000-m-high mountains and long beaches with the thundering waves of the Pacific Ocean: Canada's west coast fascinates with wild nature and unspoilt primeval landscapes.

Vancouver Island (*vancouverisland.travel*) is the largest island (450km long) on the west coast of North America and it is a world of its own. The island's rewards are in its contrasts: sleepy fishing villages, First Nation reservations and lumberjack camps in the isolated

Pacific Rim National Park

north; bustling holiday villages and the elegant capital Victoria in the south. To date, only one road leads along the whole island: Highway 19, the north–south thoroughfare. For most of its length it runs along on the eastern coast, protected by a long mountain range. And in summer, the warm waters of the Georgia Strait are quite pleasant for bathing. The wild, rainy western coast – which is home to the Pacific Rim National Park – is still almost inaccessible and thus an ideal destination for wilderness hikers and kayakers.

VANCOUVER ISLAND

Kingcome Inlet

Port Progress

Sullivan Bay

Simoom Sound

Minstrel Island

Inside Passage ★ 9 ● **Port Hardy**
p. 62

8 Alert Bay
10 Telegraph Cove

Port McNeill

Port Nevill

Port Alice

Prince of Whales ★

19

19

390km, 4.5 hrs

CANADA

20 km
12.43 mi

Long Beach

MARCO POLO HIGHLIGHTS

★ **INNER HARBOUR**
Hustle and bustle, yachts and flower pots
hanging from the street lamps ➤ p. 54

★ **INSIDE PASSAGE**
Silent fjords, deep blue water: the most
beautiful coast in all of Canada ➤ p. 62

★ **PACIFIC RIM NATIONAL PARK**
Ancient giant trees, rain forests and wild
pristine beaches along the west coast
➤ p. 58

★ **PRINCE OF WHALES**
See the pods of magnificent killer whales
➤ p. 63

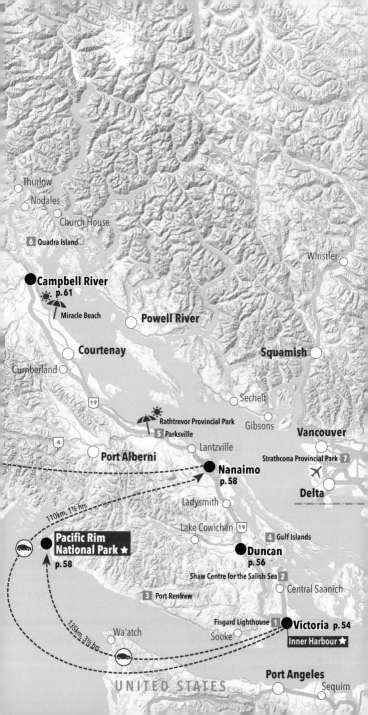

Thurlow

Nodales

Church House

6 Quadra Island

● **Campbell River**
p. 61

☀🏖 Miracle Beach

● **Powell River**

Whistler ○

○ **Courtenay**

Cumberland ○

Squamish

[19]

Sechelt ○

☀🏖 Rathtrevor Provincial Park
5 Parksville

Gibsons ○

Vancouver

[4]

○ **Port Alberni**

○ Lantzville

Strathcona Provincial Park **7**

● **Nanaimo**
p. 58

✈

Delta ○

○ Ladysmith

110km, 1½ hrs

Lake Cowichan [19]

4 Gulf Islands

**Pacific Rim
National Park** ★
p. 58

● **Duncan**
p. 56

Shaw Centre for the Salish Sea **2**

○ Central Saanich

3 Port Renfrew

135km, 3½ hrs

Wa'atch

Fisgard Lighthouse **1**

● **Victoria** p. 54

Sooke ○

Inner Harbour ★

Port Angeles

UNITED STATES

Sequim ○

VICTORIA

(📖 E15) **Victoria (pop. 370,000), the capital of British Columbia, basks in the colonial legacy of the British Empire – with landscaped public parks, Victorian architecture, double-decker buses and horse-drawn carriages for sightseeing.**

The mild climate (ideal for golf enthusiasts) and its location on the waters of the Juan de Fuca Strait make Victoria one of the most popular resorts in the west. It is now a favourite with well-heeled pensioners who want to spend their retirement playing golf. It is also popular with students and young people who enjoy sailing and who appreciate the city's leisure activities.

SIGHTSEEING

INNER HARBOUR ★
No visit to Victoria is complete without a walk along the harbour basin, filled with sailboats and yachts, to some of the city's major attractions. On the eastern side is the famed *Fairmont Empress Hotel*, built in 1906, inviting you to enjoy a traditional English tea, whereas on the northern side is the *old town* with its shopping streets and small alleyways. To the south, in a commanding position, is the magnificent *Parliament Building* dating from 1898, with a statue of Queen Victoria. The best way to explore the harbour is to take a trip on one of the small *Harbour*

INSIDER TIP
A boat trip

Ferry Company boats (round trip C$30 | departure from Empress Hotel | victoriaharbourferry.com).

ROYAL BRITISH COLUMBIA MUSEUM
The largest museum in the province: the natural history section includes a micro rain forest and a tidal pool, while the cultural section has magnificent totem poles and a longhouse of the West Coast First Nations as well as exhibitions about pioneer history. With IMAX cinema and shop. *Daily 10am–5pm | admission C$27, incl. IMAX C$37 | 675 Belleville St | royalbcmuseum.bc.ca | ⏱ 2–3 hrs*

BUTCHART GARDENS
The Queen would be delighted by the extensive historical garden around a former quarry. *Summer 8.45am–10pm, otherwise 9am–5pm | admission C$33 | 800 Benvenuto Av. | Brentwood Bay | butchartgardens.com*

BEACON HILL PARK
The famous *Trans-Canada Highway* ends here at the Pacific coast on

WHERE TO START?
Inner Harbour is the heart of the city; from here it is only a short walk to the Royal British Columbia Museum and to Parliament in the south and to the old town on Government Street and Chinatown on Fisgard Street in the north. Public parking is just north of Inner Harbour along Wharf Street.

Douglas Street, having run 7,821km all the way from Newfoundland on Canada's Atlantic coast. From here you can take the *Scenic Marine Drive* that follows the coast through parks and wealthy suburbs such as Oak Bay.

EAGLE WING TOURS

Whale watching with catamarans to the islands off the coast where several pods of orca live in summer. *3- to 4-hour tour C$135 including pick-up at the hotel | departure at Fisherman's Wharf | 12 Erie St | tel. 250 3 84 80 08 | eaglewingtours.com*

EATING & DRINKING

FLYING OTTER GRILL

Popular pub with a terrace by the harbour, surrounded by yachts and seaplanes; good for breakfast, lunch and dinner. *950 Wharf St | tel. 250 4 14 42 20 | C$$*

MO:LÉ

A cosy coffee shop offering tasty multi-cultural cuisine using many organic ingredients. Only open for breakfast and lunch. *554 Pandora Av. | tel. 250 3 85 66 53 | C$–$$*

STEAMSHIP GRILL

The most beautiful location for dining by the harbour is this magnificent art deco building. The quality of the steak and fish dishes matches that of the architecture. *470 Belleville St | tel. 778 4 33 67 36 | C$$$*

SWAN'S PUB AND CAFE

A popular pub in the city, serving

salads and fresh fish, that is also a good option for an evening out. What's more, it provides stylish accommodation on the first floor. *506 Pandora St | tel. 250 3 61 33 10 | swanshotel.com | C$*

SHOPPING

MARKET SQUARE

The brick buildings of the beautifully renovated warehouses at the harbour are full of shops, art galleries and restaurants. *560 Johnson St*

AROUND VICTORIA

1 FISGARD LIGHTHOUSE

15km / 20 mins by car from Victoria
Since 1860, the picturesque lighthouse to the west of Hwy 1A – the oldest on the Canadian west coast – has been guiding vessels into the harbour. From there, the highway continues westward to a real gourmet treat: *Sooke Harbour House (1528 Whiffen Spit Rd | Sooke | tel. 250 6 42 34 21 | sookeharbourhouse. com | €€–€€€, including 28 rooms | €€€)*. It is perfectly located on a high spot above a small cove, provides great views and serves delicious regional cuisine. *E15*

2 SHAW CENTRE FOR THE SALISH SEA

30km / 30 mins by car from Victoria
The underwater ecosystem of Canada's

west coast is the subject of this excellent, non-profit aquarium north of Victoria. *Daily 10am–5pm; winter 10am–4.30pm | admission C$17.50, children C$8 | 9811 Seaport Place | Sidney | salishcentre.org | E14*

DUNCAN

(E14) **This country town (pop. 23,000) in the fertile Cowichan Valley was nothing special until the Cowichan First Nation on the adjacent reservation founded a cultural centre to honour their traditions and began to carve totem poles. Today, the village is dotted with brightly painted poles – widely appreciated by the locals in town as they attract tourists and bring in the money.**

SIGHTSEEING

BC FOREST DISCOVERY CENTER

At this open-air museum you can explore everything that has to do with logging and *lumberjacks* – from old chainsaws and a sawmill to a real lumberjack camp. *Daily in summer 10am–4.30pm | admission C$16 including a ride on an old steam train, children C$8 | 2892 Drinkwater Rd | bcforestdiscoverycentre.com*

COWICHAN BAY MARITIME CENTRE

Boat museum spread among several small houses at the harbour. It's also a good place to visit with children. *Open in summer 8.30am–8pm | admission free | 1761 Cowichan Bay Rd | classicboats.org*

EATING & DRINKING

GENOA BAY CAFE

Located somewhat out of the way in a secluded and idyllic harbour cove, the Genoa Bay Café serves highly creative fish and meat dishes. The trip is well worth the extra time spent getting there. *5000 Genoa Bay Rd | tel. 250 7 46 76 21 | C$$*

SIDER TIP
ine dining by the harbour

AROUND DUNCAN

🔳 PORT RENFREW

100km / 1 hr and 40 mins by car from Duncan

From Duncan, take the recently opened and only partly paved Hwy 18 via Lake Cowichan and the densely forested mountains to Port Renfrew on the west coast. The small, secluded village sits on the southern edge of the *Pacific Rim National Park* (the starting point for the West Coast Trail) and offers a long beach and camping in the adjacent First Nation reservation. Don't miss the *Botanical Beach* with its bizarre rock formations and diverse marine flora found

SIDER TIP
Walk on the seabed

Totem poles by the Cowichan First Nation

in large pools formed by the tides. (Make sure to ask for the timing of the low tide). Continue on Hwy 14 from Port Renfrew to Victoria and you will have completed a round trip of the southern part of Vancouver Island. *⊞ E14*

NANAIMO

(□ E14) **Nanaimo is the northern ferry port for boats to the mainland and a good starting point for tours to the central part of the island.**

With its well-kept parks, amazing yacht harbours and an attractive harbour promenade, Nanaimo, the second-largest town (pop. 90,000) on Vancouver Island, is beautiful. Over the last few years, it has gained a reputation as a diving location. The extremely clear water gives you a great chance of discovering wrecks and diverse underwater flora.

SPORT & ACTIVITIES

WILDPLAY NANAIMO 🎭

This adventure park for both adults and children, with bungee jumps, zip lining and rope climbing, promises plenty of adrenaline. *Prices from C$30 | 35 Nanaimo River Rd | tel. 855 5 95 22 51 | wildplay.com*

AROUND NANAIMO

4 GULF ISLANDS

8km / 40 mins by ferry to Gabriola
A whole archipelago of small islands lies between Vancouver Island and the mainland. *Saltspring*, *Galiano* and *Gabriola* are the most important among them and are accessible by ferry from Swartz Bay, Crofton or Nanaimo. The wild nature and mild and sunny climate – you can even find palm trees – has attracted artists, writers and artisans.

The best way to explore the islands is by bicycle: you can travel quickly from island to island by ferry and on some of the islets – where certain parts are car-free – a bicycle is the best means of transport. *□ E–F14*

5 PARKSVILLE 🎭

25km / 30 mins by car from Nanaimo
To the north of Nanaimo you'll find warm beaches for bathing. Here, the sheltered Strait of Georgia is shallow so that the water warms up quickly around the extended sandbanks of *Parksville* and *Qualicum Beach* as well as in 🌴 *Rathtrevor Provincial Park*. For an excellent organic lunch visit the *Bread & Honey Food Co. (162 Harrison Av. | tel. 250 5 86 10 21 | €)*. A 20-minute drive inland on Hwy 4 leads to the *MacMillan Provincial Park* where you can marvel at the 800-year-old Douglas firs and cedar trees or the cascades of *Little Qualicum Falls* (hiking trails). *□ E14*

PACIFIC RIM NAT. PARK

(□ D–E14) **Some of the wildest and most beautiful sections of the coast form part of the 400-km² ★ 🌴 *Pacific Rim National Park*. The park protects ancient rain forest, rugged cliffs and driftwood-strewn beaches,**

such as the 11-km-long and in parts 100-m-wide *Long Beach*.

The *Kwisitis Centre* on *Wickaninnish Beach* provides very detailed and competent information on the natural history of the region. The friendly and helpful rangers will give you valuable tips for hikes. The nature trails, such as the *Rainforest Trail*, are particularly impressive. Given the weather conditions in the area it is a good idea to equip yourself with a waterproof cape.

It is also very popular to go bear watching from a boat. This is a safe way to observe the predators. Accommodation and tours are offered in the harbour towns of *Tofino* and *Ucluelet* at the northern and southern edges of the park respectively.

SIGHTSEEING

REMOTE PASSAGES

Trips by motorboat and rubber dinghy to observe grey whales, orcas and bears and also to the hot springs on a secluded island. *51 Wharf St | tel. 250 7 25 33 30 | remotepassages.com*

BARKLEY SOUND SERVICE

A former Norwegian freight ferry offers cruises in the Barkley Sound. Full-day trips from Port Alberni to Ucluelet and Bamfield. They also take hikers to the *West Coast Trail* and kayakers to the *Broken Group Islands*. The small archipelago is a dream destination for wild kayaking. *Port Alberni | tel. 250 7 23 83 13 | ladyrosemarine.com*

Encounter black bears in the Clayoquot Sound in the Pacific Rim National Park

Migrating salmon: Campbell River is known as the "salmon capital of the world"

ATLEO RIVER AIR SERVICE
Organised tours by seaplane across glaciers, fjords and waterfalls. *50 Wingen Lane | tel. 866 6 62 85 36 | atleoair.com*

EATING & DRINKING

NORWOODS
Creative west coast cuisine in a cosy restaurant decorated with lots of wood. The ingredients, such as mussels or *Dungeness crab*, are supplied by local fishermen. *1714 Peninsula Rd | Ucluelet | tel. 250 7 26 70 01 | C$$–$$$*

SHELTER
Try the salmon and halibut in a Macadamia crust, or the pork chops in apple sauce. Excellent also is the *Dungeness crab*, fresh from the west coast. *601 Campbell St | tel. 250 7 25 33 53 | C$$*

SOBO
Delicious and healthy west coast cuisine. The lunchtime menu is very reasonably priced. *311 Neill St | tel. 250 7 25 23 41 | C$$–$$$*

TACOFINO
Fabulous Mexican burritos and tacos from a food truck for surfers. If you prefer chips, go next door to the *Wildside Grill*, an equally good fish & chip shop with ultra-fresh fish – one of the owners is a local fisherman. *1184 Pacific Rim Hwy | Tofino | tel. 250 7 26 82 88 | C$*

INSIDER TIP *Freshly caught*

SPORT & ACTIVITIES

SURF SISTER
Ride a wave for an exciting adrenaline rush: in spite of the name, they offer both mixed and women-only courses. A trial session, including board and *wetsuit*, costs about C$90. *625 Campbell St | tel. 250 7 25 44 56 | surfsister.com*

TOFINO SEA KAYAKING
To truly understand the west coast, you have to experience it from the water. Kayaking is ideal for this purpose and, with a bit of luck, you may be able to spot black bears. Experienced guides and robust kit. Half-day tour from

C$70. *320 Main St | tel. 250 7 25 42 22 | tofinoseakayaking.com*

WEST COAST TRAIL

If you want to hike in the wilderness and are reasonably fit, you can venture on a five- to seven-day trip *(booking required | tel. 519 8 26 53 91)* on this 72-km-long trail from Port Renfrew to Bamfield. The trail, which was originally created as a rescue track for shipwrecked sailors, winds along the beaches and cliffs of the dramatic and rugged coastline.

WILD PACIFIC TRAIL ✦

This well-maintained hiking trail consists of several legs of 1–2 hours each. It runs along the coast by the southern town of Ucluelet and offers breathtaking views of the ocean across the cliffs and coves.

CAMPBELL RIVER

(□ E13) **This port city (pop. 35,000), among the largest on Vancouver Island, is an anglers' paradise.**

The biggest salmon in Canada are caught in the central part of the island; king salmon weighing 30kg are not uncommon. Young salmon can be watched in the *Quinsam River Hatchery (4217 Argonaut Rd)*, approx. 5km north of the town, and in the nearby stream adult salmon return from the sea in August. This is also the time of the famous ⚑ *Salmon Festival*.

To the south of the town there are beautiful provincial parks, such as 🏕 *Miracle Beach*, with beaches stretching along the Strait of Georgia.

AROUND CAMPBELL RIVER

6 QUADRA ISLAND

8km / 30 mins by ferry

This offshore island is a Kwakiutl First Nation reservation. Here you will find the *Nuyumbalees Cultural Centre (daily in summer 10am–5pm | admission C$10 | Cape Mudge)*, a true treasure trove of Native American masks. If you want to stay overnight, then try the *Tsa-Kwa-Luten Lodge (35 rooms | tel. 250 8 30 22 99 | capemudgeresort.bc.ca, with camp-site)*, run by tribe members and decorated with carvings. *□ E13*

7 STRATHCONA PROV. PARK

50km / 1 hr by car from Campbell River

The oldest provincial park in British Columbia is especially interesting for hikers. It has a well-developed net-work of paths leading from the two roads in the park up into the alpine regions. At 2,500m *Golden Hinde* is the highest mountain. Particularly beautiful is the hike to *Flower Ridge* at the southern end of *Buttle Lake*.

On the banks of the Upper Campbell Lake is the cosy 🏨

Strathcona Park Lodge (tel. 250 2 86 31 22 | strathconaparklodge. com | C$$) which, as well as accommodation, offers hiking, mountaineering and canoeing courses for teenagers. 🔲 D–E 13–14

PORT HARDY

(🔲 D12–13) **The busy port is evidence that the town (pop. 4,000), in the wild north of Vancouver Island, is an important fishing base.**
Port Hardy is liked by visitors as it is a good starting point for the *Inside Passage* and other rewarding trips: you can see whales, bears and eagles on kayak trips, hike to Cape Scott and enjoy flights and boat trips.

SIGHTSEEING

GREAT BEAR LODGE
A floating eco lodge that is the base for grizzly bear and nature observation tours. Great location in a fjord on the mainland coast. Access is by seaplane from Port Hardy. Tel. 250 9 49 94 96 | greatbeartours.com

AROUND PORT HARDY

🔳 ALERT BAY
40km / approx. 2 hrs incl. ferry crossing from Port McNeill
The village (pop. 600) on a small

offshore island to the south on Hwy 19 is home to the Kwakwaka'wakw First Nation *(Kwakiutl)* who are famous for their expressive carving. The most beautiful heirlooms of the tribe – old masks, decorated chests and totem poles – are exhibited in the *U' Mista Cultural Centre (daily in summer 9am–5pm, otherwise Tue–Sat | admission C$12 | umista.ca | guided tours organised by the Culture Shock Gallery by the ferry port | tel. 250 9 74 24 84).* For a night right on the river, try the *Seine Boat Inn (10 rooms | tel. 877 3 34 94 65 | seineboatinn.com | C$–$$).* 🔲 D13

> **INSIDER TIP**
> **First Nation heritage**

🔳 INSIDE PASSAGE ★ 🏖
The 500-km-long coastal shipping route runs along the west coast and was once the route followed by of thousands of adventurers on their way to the gold fields of Klondike and to Alaska. There are still no roads along the coast, which is lined by numerous fjords. The only way to experience the legendary route is by cruise ship (from

Inside Passage: legendary waterway along the west coast of British Columbia

Vancouver) or on one of the *BC Ferries* on a 15-hour trip between *Port Hardy* and *Prince Rupert*. (You will need to book several months in advance, information on *tel. 888 2 23 37 79 | bcferries.com)* ⌗ *D–E 12–14*

⑩ TELEGRAPH COVE

65km / 1 hr by car from Port Hardy
The former fishing hamlet (pop. 20) south of Port Hardy is now a mecca for whale watchers and researchers. Several groups of orca live here in the salmon-rich waters of a marine reserve (between the mainland and Vancouver Island) where they can be seen throughout the summer. Half-day boat tours to Johnstone Strait, an Orca reserve, are on offer between May and October with ★ *Prince of Whales (Telegraph Cove | C$130 | tel. 888 3 83 48 84 | princeofwhales.com).*

Also, full-day boat trips are offered from Telegraph Cove to see the grizzlies in *Knight Inlet*. The bears can often be seen up close from a boat in the secluded fjord near the mainland.

Tours are organised by *Tide Rip Tours (day tour C$300–370 | tel. 250 3 39 53 20 | grizzlycanada.com)* from mid-May to September. ⌗ *D13*

BRITISH COLUMBIA

BETWEEN THE ROCKIES & THE PACIFIC

British Columbia (or BC) boastfully calls itself the most scenic province in Canada. And not without reason: the westernmost region of the country offers the greatest variety of landscapes as well as the best opportunities for an adventure holiday.

Whether canoeing, hiking, heli-skiing, fishing or biking, BC has thrills and adventure to suit every taste. It even has sunny beaches – such as the ones around the lakes in the Okanagan Valley. The entire region is characterised by large mountain ranges, alternating with

Rogers Pass

high plateaus. Only the northeast around Dawson Creek is flat. There, the province extends to the foothills of the prairies. And on the border with the United States at Osoyoos, you will find Canada's only desert – it even includes cacti and rattlesnakes.

The mainland of this large province covers approx. 950,000km², almost four times the size of the United Kingdom. As such, Vancouver Island (see page 50) and the city of Vancouver (see page 38) each deserve their own chapter.

BRITISH COLUMBIA

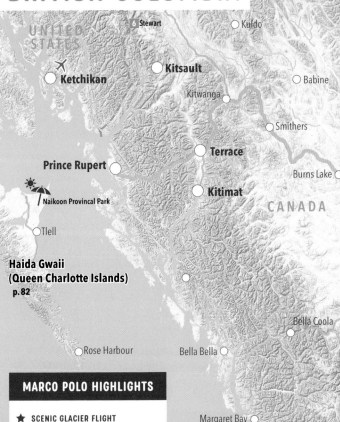

6 Stewart
○ Kuldo

○ Ketchikan

● Kitsault

○ Babine

Kitwanga ○

○ Smithers

● Terrace

Burns Lake ○

● Prince Rupert

● Kitimat

CANADA

Naikoon Provincal Park

○ Tlell

**Haida Gwaii
(Queen Charlotte Islands)**
p. 82

○

Bella Coola ○

○ Rose Harbour

Bella Bella ○

MARCO POLO HIGHLIGHTS

★ **SCENIC GLACIER FLIGHT**
Admire the icy peaks of the Coast
Mountains from the air ➤ p. 69

Margaret Bay ○

★ **MISSION HILL WINERY**
Canada's answer to the wineries of
Europe ➤ p. 73

Port Hardy ○

★ **WILDFLOWER MEADOWS ON
MOUNT REVELSTOKE**
A blaze of alpine colour, but only at the
height of summer ➤ p. 77

★ **HELMCKEN FALLS**
Spectacular waterfall in the midst of
verdant nature ➤ p. 79

★ **FORT ST JAMES**
Gain an insight into the hard lives of the
fur traders 150 years ago ➤ p. 81

100 km
62.14 mi

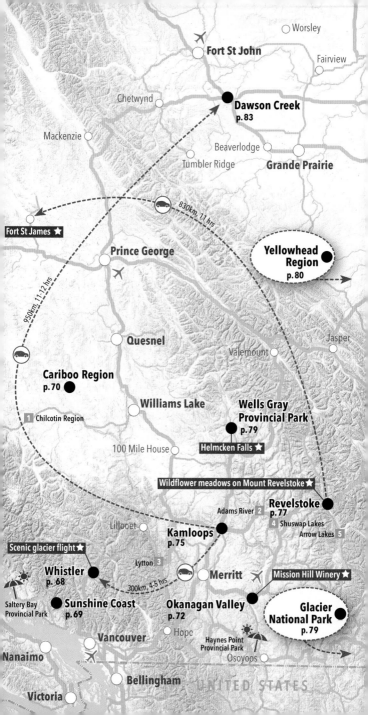

Worsley

Fort St John

Fairview

Chetwynd

Dawson Creek
p.83

Mackenzie

Beaverlodge

Tumbler Ridge

Grande Prairie

830km, 11 hrs

Fort St James ★

Prince George

950km, 11-12 hrs

**Yellowhead
Region**
p.80

Jasper

Quesnel

Valemount

Cariboo Region
p.70

Williams Lake

**Wells Gray
Provincial Park**
p.79

1 Chilcotin Region

Helmcken Falls ★

100 Mile House

Wildflower meadows on Mount Revelstoke ★

Revelstoke
p.77

Adams River 2

Lillooet

4 Shuswap Lakes

Arrow Lakes 5

Scenic glacier flight ★

Kamloops
p.75

Lytton 3

Whistler
p. 68

Merritt

Mission Hill Winery ★

Saltery Bay
Provincial Park

Sunshine Coast
p.69

300km, 4-5 hrs

Okanagan Valley
p.72

**Glacier
National Park**
p.79

Vancouver

Hope

Haynes Point
Provincial Park

Nanaimo

Osoyoos

Bellingham

UNITED STATES

Victoria

WHISTLER

The sophisticated winter sports resort (pop. 12,000), about two hours' drive north of Vancouver, was the venue for the alpine events of the 2010 Winter Olympics.

It is hard to believe that this small, but now world-famous town in the snowy *Coast Mountains* was only founded about 50 years ago. However, with two mountains, *Whistler* and *Blackcomb*, and nearly 40 ski lifts it is a superb ski resort. Some of the lifts also operate in the summer, making it easy to walk, bike or go glacier skiing in the summit region. In the valley below, life plays out around the busy pedestrian zone of *Whistler Village* lined with shops, restaurants and cafés.

The journey to Whistler is worthwhile in itself. The *Sea to Sky Highway* (Hwy 99), which provides fabulous views across Howe Sound, winds along the shores of a deep fjord. There are several viewing points, numerous spectacular waterfalls and you can take a cable-car ride near Squamish. Information boards outline the history of the First Nations in this region. *F13*

Enjoy the snow on the mountains around Whistler in winter and its glaciers in summer

SIGHTSEEING

AUDAIN ART MUSEUM

The private British Columbian art collection ranges from Native American to modern styles. The museum opened in 2016 and the building itself is worth a visit too. *Wed–Mon 9am–5pm, Thu/Fri until 7pm | admission C$18 | 4350 Blackcomb Way*

BC MINING MUSEUM 👯

Old tunnels, jackhammers, panning for gold and a giant truck are the attractions at this museum which is housed in an old copper mine. *Daily in summer 9am–5.30pm | admission (guided tour) C$30, children C$19 | on Hwy 99 at Britannia Beach | ⏱ 2 hrs*

HARBOUR AIR SEAPLANES

Genuinely Canadian: a ★ *scenic glacier flight* in seaplanes from Green Lake to the icy peaks of the Coast Mountains. *C$120–370 | 8069 Nicklaus North Blvd | tel. 800 6 65 02 12 | harbourair.com*

EATING & DRINKING

INGRID'S VILLAGE CAFE 🐖

Centrally placed and popular with local people: good soups, burgers and chops. *4305 Village Stroll | tel. 604 9 32 70 00 | C$*

STEEP'S GRILL

Restaurant by the Whistler Mountain cable car station at an altitude of 1,850m and with wonderful views of the Coast Mountains. *Tel. 604 9 05 23 79 | C$$*

TABLE NINETEEN

You don't have to be a golfer to enjoy Whistler's most beautiful terrace on the shores of Green Lake. However, a beer will surely taste even better after a round on the championship course next door. *8080 Nicklaus North Blvd | tel. 604 9 38 98 98 | C$$*

SUNSHINE COAST

Sunshine Coast is protected by a series of small islands and its climate is therefore very sunny and mild. It lies north of Vancouver and is perfect for a several-day trip to explore the verdant fjord landscape by the Pacific.

Hwy 101 winds 140km along the coastal bays northwards until the road ends in *Lund*. Lining the way are marinas and sleepy fishing villages – often home to artists and people living an alternative lifestyle – and coastal parks such as the 🏕 *Saltery Bay Provincial Park* (with campsites). The fishing village of *Egmont* is the start of the impressive 4-km-long hike to the *Skookumchuck Narrows* – where the tide forces seawater through the narrows, creating some of the world's fastest tidal rapids and gigantic whirlpools. For information on the best times to visit, go to *secheltvisitor centre.com/skookumchuck-narrows.* ▢ *E13–14*

INSIDER TIP
Forces of nature at work

SPORT & ACTIVITIES

SONORA RESORT
Luxurious and eco-friendly holiday resort in a dream location on an isolated island. Bear watching, fishing, hiking trails and a great spa. Accessible by boat or seaplane. *88 rooms| Sonora Island | tel. 604 2 33 04 60 | sonora resort.com | C$$$*

SUNSHINE COAST TOURS
Guided tours, water taxis and boat trips to the Princess Louisa Inlet and to the Skookumchuck Narrows are offered by *Sunshine Coast Tours (4289 Orca Rd | Garden Bay | tel. 800 8 70 90 55 | sunshinecoasttours.ca).*

CARIBOO REGION

The steppe-like plateau on the upper reaches of the Fraser River (landwithoutlimits.com) is Canada's own Wild West: hilly ranch country with large herds of cattle and gold rush towns.

To supply miners during the great gold rush of 1860, the *Cariboo Wagon Road* was the first road to be built in Western Canada. Hwy 97 follows this old route from the south. Many of the small ranch villages were named after the distances from the original start of the road in *Lillooet (𝄞 E13): 70 Mile House, 100 Mile House,* etc. The starting point for tours around *Barkerville, Likely* or *Horsefly* is *Williams Lake*

(𝄞 F12) which hosts a rodeo on 1 July each year. *𝄞 F–G 11–13*

SIGHTSEEING

BARKERVILLE 👥
During the 1870 gold rush, Barkerville was the biggest city north of San Francisco. Today, a wonderfully nostalgic museum village remains with Western façades, wooden boardwalks and actors who bring the pioneer era to life. The restaurants aren't bad either: the historic *Wake-up Jake Café (tel. 250 9 94 32 59 | C$)* serves hearty gold-digger food and delicious pancakes for breakfast, and the *Lung Duck Tong Restaurant (tel. 250 9 94 34 58 | C$)* offers good Chinese dishes. *Visitor centre with museum | daily 8.30am–6pm, village until 8pm | in summer admission C$14.50 | at the end of Hwy 26 | barkerville.ca | ⏱ 4 hrs | 𝄞 H11*

COTTONWOOD HOUSE
A historic site in Cottonwood, a faithfully restored coaching inn dating back to 1864, also horse-drawn carriage rides. *Daily in summer 10am–5pm | admission free | on Hwy 26 | 𝄞 G11*

WELLS
The old mining town on the western edge of the Cariboo Mountains has evolved into an arts centre for the young, creative and environmentally conscious, with galleries and theatres. In summer, bands make frequent appearances at festivals and you can make the acquaintance of talented

Encountering a moose at close quarters

actors within the creative scene, for example at *Island Mountain Arts (2323 Pooley St | support-imarts.com).* ⎕ *G11*

SPORT & ACTIVITIES

BECKER'S LODGE
Lodge right on the lake, also chalets and camping. Equipment and rental for the week-long canoe trips on the well-known Bowron Lakes. *7 log cabins | Wells | tel. 250 9 92 88 64 | beckerslodge.ca | ⎕ G11*

ECOTOURS-BC
Simple wilderness lodge deep in the hinterland of the Cariboo Mountains, an hour's drive east of Williams Lake. Grizzly bear-watching tours

INSIDER TIP
Bears ahead!

along the local salmon streams, respecting the rules of nature conservation. *Likely | tel. 250 7 90 22 92 | ecotours-bc.com | ⎕ G12*

AROUND CARIBOO REGION

◼ CHILCOTIN REGION
450km / 8 hrs by car from Cariboo
If you are at Williams Lake and wish to go deeper into the wilderness, take a trip into the backcountry on Hwy 20. It leads west through the ranch region of Chilcotin, where forest fires raged in the summer of 2017, and through

the massive, still undeveloped *Tweedsmuir Provincial Park* (campsites, trails) up to the coast at *Bella Coola* – a perfect destination for anglers and wilderness hikers. Not far from here is where Alexander MacKenzie reached the Pacific in 1793 – Canada's first transcontinental crossing. From Bella Coola, a *BC Ferries* boat travels several times a week (booking is essential).

The log cabins of *Tweedsmuir Park Lodge (Hwy 20 | Tweedsmuir Park | tel. 604 9 05 49 94 | tweedsmuirpark lodge.com)* make a good starting point for bear watching. They also offer guided boat tours during the salmon season. 🕮 *D–F10–12*

OKANAGAN VALLEY

The valley is defined by an elongated chain of lakes and, due to its mild climate, orchards and vineyards have sprung up, and it's also a popular recreation and holiday spot.

The conditions in the Okanagan Valley are well suited to vineyards: sandy soil and hot, dry summers. Even ice wine (wine from grapes frozen on the vine) does very well here, as winter usually arrives quite abruptly with icy temperatures. Today, there are 120 wineries cultivating grapes in and around the Okanagan Valley. The main varietals include: Zweigelt, Viognier and Pinot Gris, but also Merlot and Cabernet Sauvignon. In some places, such as the *Naramatha Bench* area near Penticton, there is one winery after the other, most of them offering tastings. The wineries that are scattered throughout the whole valley today produce some excellent wines – after more than 40 years of experimentation – and are well worth a visit.

The southern end of the valley is extremely dry, even cacti grow there, but the slopes around the lakes burst into a blaze of glory in spring, when the apple, cherry and peach trees blossom. In summer and autumn you can buy honey, jam, cider and of course fresh fruit at roadside stalls. On the eastern shore of the approximately 150-km-long Okanagan Lake is the main town of *Kelowna* (pop. 127,000), where the mild temperatures attract

many pensioners who spend their days playing golf and tennis. *H14*

SIGHTSEEING

GRAY MONK ESTATE WINERY

This is where you can learn all about Canadian wine: guided tours, followed by wine tasting and some spectacular views of the lake. Excellent restaurant *Grapevine* with panoramic view. *Daily in summer 10am–7pm, tours Mon–Fri 11am, 2pm and 4pm | admission C$20 | 12055 Camp Rd | Lake Country | graymonk.com*

MISSION HILL WINERY ★

A magnificent Tuscan-inspired estate high up on the hill that is surrounded by vineyards and orchards. It is the most important winery in the Okanagan Valley and it has a restaurant on the terrace. *Daily in summer 10am–8pm, otherwise 10am–6pm | guided tour C$20 | 1730 Mission Hill Rd | West Bank | missionhillwinery. com*

NK'MIP CELLARS

Moving with the times, the ultra-modern winery and cultural centre of the Osoyoos First Nation features impressive architecture. Its construction incorporates many sustainable elements of the indigenous people. The centre has a restaurant that serves organic food, a large resort with golf course and a campsite. *Daily in summer 9am–8pm, otherwise until 5pm | admission free | guided tours (daily*

INSIDER TIP
First Nation building design

The Mission Hill Winery produces superb wines

Beach life by two large lakes in the Okanagan Valley

2pm and 4pm) C$10 | 1400 Rancher Creek Rd | Osoyoos | nkmipcellars.com

O'KEEFE RANCH

Established in 1867, the cattle ranch was once the largest in British Columbia. Today, it is an open-air museum and its restored ranch house, post office, church and blacksmith provide vivid insights into the life of the early pioneers. *Daily in summer 10am–5pm | admission C$13.50, children C$10 | 9km north of Vernon on Hwy 97 | 2 hrs*

EATING & DRINKING

EARLS ON TOP RESTAURANT

Enjoy fish, steak and pasta on the shores of the lake, with terrace. *211 Bernard Av. | Kelowna | tel. 250 7 63 27 77 | C$$*

QUAILS' GATE ESTATE WINERY

Wine shop and elegant terrace restaurant with lake views. Very good for lunch with trout or wild boar loin on the menu. *3303 Boucherie Rd | West Bank | tel. 250 7 69 44 51 | quailsgate. com | C$$$*

SALTY'S BEACH HOUSE

A popular fish restaurant on the beach of Okanagan Lake. *1000 Lakeshore Dr. | Penticton | tel. 250 4 93 50 01 | C$$*

SPORT & ACTIVITIES

PENTICTON CHANNEL

Tubing is the name given to the watery fun of drifting down the channel between both lakes in Penticton in big inflatable tubes. *Coyote Cruises (tel. 250 4 92 21 15)* provides the tubes (for approx. C$12) and also organises the return journey. *Hwy 97 at the northern end of the channel | coyote cruises.ca*

WILDHORSE MOUNTAIN RANCH

Experience a cowboy holiday on this B&B ranch in an idyllic valley west of Okanagan Lake. Daily horse rides. *7 rooms | 25808 Wildhorse Rd | Summerland | tel. 250 4 94 05 06 | wildhorsemountainranch.com | C$–$$*

BEACHES

Beautiful beaches, such as those in the 🛶 *Haynes Point Provincial Park*, are found in the southern part of the valley near *Osoyoos* and in *Penticton*. If you are here in early August, you can visit the peach festival.

DINING LIKE A TRAPPER?

In a nature-loving and wildlife-rich country such as Canada one would expect to see more tasty wild duck or juicy moose steak on the menu. Not a bit of it! By law, all privately shot game may only be consumed privately, whereas wild game for restaurants must come from a farm. So Canadians hunt exclusively for personal consumption, and you can only enjoy wild game by private invitation. The hunting season is in the autumn and by the time the next visitors arrive in the spring, the Wapiti steaks will have long since been eaten.

WELLNESS

SPARKLING HILL RESORT

Super luxurious, environmentally friendly hotel that belongs to the Swarovski crystal family. The highlight: the 3.5 million crystals that were incorporated into the spectacular design. There is also the elegant and contemplative *KurSpa* with an invigorating cold sauna and maple syrup treatments. *149 rooms | 888 Sparkling Place | Vernon | tel. 250 2 75 15 56 | sparklinghill.com | C$$$*

KAMLOOPS

Kamloops is the third largest city in the province (pop. 90,000) but is not all that impressive by itself. However, since it is located at the crossroads of major highways and features some large shopping malls, this city is a good place to stock up on supplies before starting on a trip into the hinterland.

The centrally located *Victoria Street* has seen a revival in recent years. You will find plenty of shops and restaurants that are definitely worth a visit. The *Riverside Park* on the banks of the Thompson River with its big 🛝 children's playground is a good place to relax. *▥ G13*

SIGHTSEEING

BC WILDLIFE PARK 🛝

Lynx, caribou, cougar and mountain goat: in this park you have a good opportunity to get close to the rare wild animals of Western Canada – especially as they are protected in a way that is appropriate for the species. *Daily in summer 9.30am–5pm | admission C$16, children C$12 | 9077 Dallas Dr. | bcwildlife.org |* ⏱ *2–3 hrs*

EATING & DRINKING

COMMODORE GRAND

This is a brewery pub and entertainment venue for the younger crowd in the old town. It serves good salads, steaks and pizza. Live music starts after 10pm. *369 Victoria St | tel. 250 8 51 31 00 | C$–$$*

SHOPPING

ABERDEEN MALL

You can shop for hours in this huge shopping mall on the west side of the city. Good shops are The Bay, SportChek and Dolson's Sports. *1320 West Trans-Canada Hwy*

FARMERS' MARKET

Every Wednesday and Saturday the inner city hosts a farmers' market under white gazebos.

AROUND KAMLOOPS

🞵 RIVER

70km / 1 hr by car from Kamloops
All along the west coast, the salmon swim upstream to spawn, and you can experience a spectacular *salmon run* in early October in the Adams River north-east of Kamloops. Several hundreds of thousands of bright red *sockeye salmon* jostle through water that is only knee-deep. Every fourth year is a peak year: within a period of two weeks, more than two million salmon come to spawn and die. This event is happening in 2022 and again in 2026. 🕮 *G13*

🞵 LYTTON

150km / 2 hrs by car from Kamloops
The tiny village (pop. 400) to the south-west, at the confluence of the Thompson and Fraser rivers, is a popular starting point for whitewater rafting trips. South of the town is the impressive gorge where the Fraser River starts on its 100-km journey through the Coast Mountains. At *Hell's Gate*, the narrowest part of the gorge, about 50km south of Lytton, a cable car runs down to the riverbank, where, in the summer, you can watch salmon fight their way upstream through the whirlpools. *Kumsheen Rafting Adventures (on Hwy 1 | tel. 250 4 55 22 96 or tel. 800 6 63 66 67 | kumsheen.com)* offer rafting on the Thompson and Fraser rivers. 🕮 *G13*

🞵 SHUSWAP LAKES

80km / 1 hr by car from Kamloops
The large lake actually has four bodies of water; it is a popular recreation area for water sports enthusiasts. Shuswap Lake itself has more than 1,000km of untouched and densely forested shoreline. In the small villages such as *Salmon Arm* or *Sicamous* you can rent

a houseboat and explore the labyrinth of creeks and coves in your own time. *Twin Anchors Houseboat Vacations | 200 Old Town Rd W | Sicamous | tel. 250 8 36 24 50 | twinanchors.com.* ⌖ *H13*

REVELSTOKE

Revelstoke is located at the northern end of the elongated chain of lakes on the Columbia River. July to early September, high above the railway town, the ★ wild flower meadows on Mount Revelstoke are in bloom – it's an unforgettable sight. About 100 wild flower species grow around the summit.

In the town (pop. 8,500) you will find restaurants, hotels and campsites.

Access to Revelstoke National Park is easy: a gravel road leads to the 1,938-m-high *Mount Revelstoke* (in midsummer a shuttle bus is available). At the summit are some lovely short hiking trails, while down below in the valley the *Giant Cedars Trail* – which leads from the Trans-Canada Highway through dense forests of centuries-old cedars and Douglas fir trees – is also worth a hike. ⌖ *H13*

INSIDER TIP
Primeval forests

SIGHTSEEING

REVELSTOKE DAM VISITOR CENTRE

The modern visitor centre *(daily in summer 10am–4pm | admission C$6 | info tel. 250 8 14 66 97)*, 5km north of the town, explains the role of the dam

The Shuswap Lakes are ideal for a houseboat holiday

The Selkirk Mountains in the Glacier National Park are a wintery dream

on the Columbia River. Technically minded people can travel 150km further upstream to the mighty *Mica Dam*.

REVELSTOKE RAILWAY MUSEUM

The museum's showpiece is one of Canada's largest ever steam locomotives. *Daily in summer 9am–5pm, otherwise Thu–Sun 11am–4pm | admission C$10, children C$5 | 719 Track St | ⏱ 2 hrs*

AROUND REVELSTOKE

5 ARROW LAKES

170km / 3 hrs by car from Revelstoke to Sandon

On Highways 23 and 6 you can explore the largely unpopulated region and historic towns like *Kaslo*, hot springs such as *Nakusp Hot Springs* and ghost towns like *Sandon*, where dilapidated façades tell of

INSIDER TIP
Silver-diggers ghost town

the silver- and lead-mining era around 1900. 🐖 Free car ferries service the towns along the lake shore. *⊞ H13–14*

GLACIER NAT. PARK

Numerous black bears and grizzlies live in the 1,350-km² reserve in the glacier-capped *Selkirk Mountains*. Hwy 1 winds for miles through various passes in the park, protected from avalanches in winter by tunnels. At an altitude of 1,327m, on *Rogers Pass* a memorial commemorates the completion of the *Trans-Canada Highway* in 1962.

You can find valuable tips for hiking routes in the *visitor centre* next to the pass – but beware, it often rains along the western flank of the mountains! The exhibits in the visitor centre explain the painstaking construction of the railway 100 years ago. Accommodation and restaurants are to be found in the old railway village of *Golden* (pop. 4,100) at the eastern entrance to the park. *⊞ H–J13*

SIGHTSEEING

NORTHERN LIGHTS WOLF CENTRE

This privately run conservation centre has an enclosure with a pack of grey wolves, which you can view here at close quarters. Amateur photographers are given the opportunity to walk with the freely roaming predators. *Daily in summer 9am–7pm | admission C$12 | 1745 Short Rd | Golden | northernlightswildlife.com*

INSIDER TIP Walking with wolves

SPORT & ACTIVITIES

GLACIER RAFT COMPANY

Half- and full-day rafting trips with sturdy rubber boats on the Kicking Horse River. *1509 Lafontaine Rd | Golden | tel. 250 3 44 65 21 | glacierraft.com*

KICKING HORSE GONDOLA

Golden's ski resort is not only attractive in winter for skiing. In summer, you can reach the summit by cable car and hike along two fixed-rope routes, then dine at the highest restaurant in Canada. *Gondola ride C$41 | 1500 Kicking Horse Trail | tel. 800 2 58 76 69*

WELLS GRAY PROV. PARK

This provincial park on the northern edge of the Columbia Mountains stretches across an impressive 5,000km². It is pure unspoilt forest wilderness, well known for its many spectacular waterfalls, such as the 137-m-tall ★ Helmcken Falls which plunge into a narrow valley.

Just as spectacular is *Spahats Creek* that tumbles down a 120-m-deep gorge near the park entrance.

The Helmcken Falls are the main attraction of the Wells Gray Provincial Park

Wilderness hikers can explore the reserve on the wide network of hiking trails, and the *Clearwater* and *Azure Lake* chain of lakes are ideal for canoe trips. ⌕ *G–H 11–12*

SPORT & ACTIVITIES

CLEARWATER LAKE TOURS

Good canoe rentals and trips on the large, secluded lakes of the Wells Gray Provincial Park. The company also provides camping equipment for canoe and kayak tours lasting several days. *Clearwater | tel. 250 6 74 21 21 | clearwaterlaketours.com*

YELLOWHEAD REGION

The *Yellowhead Highway 16* was opened in 1970 and, apart from the Trans-Canada Highway further to the south, is the second major east-west highway in Western Canada.

The highway starts in the prairies and runs via Edmonton and Jasper through the isolated north to the Pacific. It follows the old pack route of the fur traders and provides access to the far north of British Columbia. The road is named after a fair-haired fur

'KSAN HISTORICAL VILLAGE

An open-air museum village of the Git'ksan tribe, with totem poles, carving workshops and dance performances in summer. *Daily in summer 10am–5pm | admission C$5 | guided tour C$15 | Hazelton | 🕮 E9*

TOWNS ALONG YELLOWHEAD HIGHWAY

From the border to Alberta, in Jasper National Park, the highway first crosses the dense forests of the Fraser Plateau. West of the logging town of *Prince George* (pop. 76,000, 🕮 F10–11) the route passes an extensive lake district up to the Coast Mountains where the region of the Northwest Coast First Nations begins. At *Moricetown Canyon* on the Bulkley River you can watch them fishing salmon in the traditional way during July and August.

Nearby, in the *Hazelton* (🕮 E9) area are the reservation villages of the Tsimshian

INSIDER TIP
Original totem poles

First Nation, with ancient totem poles that attest to their woodcrafting skills. In many cases, the poles are still in their original locations, for example in the villages of Kispiox and Kitwanga.

The important fishing, coal and grain port of *Prince Rupert* (pop. 15,000, 🕮 C10) is located at the western end of the *Yellowhead Highway*. It provides access to the ferry system along the west coast: the *BC Ferries* run from here south to Vancouver Island; the ships of *Alaska Marine Highway* run northwards to Alaska.

trader whose image is still shown today on the road signs. 🕮 C–G 9–11

SIGHTSEEING

FORT ST JAMES ★ 🚩 🏛

The fur-trading post, founded by Simon Fraser in 1806, has been restored and is now an excellent museum village that really brings to life the era of the fur traders. In summer you can even spend the night in the historic *Officer's House (tel. 250 9 96 71 91 | pc.gc.ca/stjames | C$$ incl. food). Daily in summer 9am–5pm | admission C$8, free for children | 50km north of Vanderhoof on Hwy 27 |* ⊙ *2 hrs |* 🕮 F10

PRINCE RUPERT ADVENTURE TOURS

The company organises half- and full-day boat excursions to watch whales and grizzly bears in the Khuzemateen reserve. *215 Cow Bay Rd | Prince Rupert | tel. 250 6 27 91 66 | adventuretours.net*

AROUND YELLOWHEAD REGION

6 STEWART

250km / 4 hrs by car from Kitwanga

Take the *Cassiar Highway* from Kitwanga for a detour into the mountainous region on the border with Alaska up to the town of Stewart at the end of a 145-km-long fjord.

Alaska begins in *Hyder*, a pleasantly scruffy little town where the bars never close. In *Fish Creek*, on the outskirts of Hyder, the silver salmon spawn in the summer and you can often see bears and bald eagles as they gorge on the fish.

In fine weather, the dirt road along Fish Creek leads a good 30km further up into the mountains with some splendid views of the gigantic Salmon Glacier. *D8*

INSIDER TIP
Icy views

HAIDA GWAII (QUEEN CHARLOTTE ISLANDS)

"Haida Gwaii", the frequently storm-tossed and rainy archipelago, formerly the home of the indigenous warlike Haida people, is now known by its original name *(lovehaidagwaii.com)* and is a genuine "Galapagos of the North" with rain forests, sea lions, bald eagles and an incredible abundance of marine creatures.

The northern *Graham Island* has a good road infrastructure (and a ferry from Prince Rupert). The north coast in the ✿ *Naikoon Provincial Park* has long and deserted beaches full of mussels and crabs. A large part of the almost uninhabited southern *Moresby Island* and its unique eco-system is now part of the *Gwaii Haanas National Park* and is only accessible by boat, kayak and seaplane. ⟼ *B9–11*

SIGHTSEEING

HAIDA HERITAGE CENTRE

Carving college of the Haida First Nation with exhibitions of totem poles and canoes. *Daily in summer 9am-6pm, Thu–Sat until 8pm | admission C$16 | Skidegate | haidaheritage centre.com*

BLUEWATER ADVENTURES

The company offers five- to eleven-day kayaking trips along the west coast, including the Queen Charlotte Islands. *3252 E 1st St | North Vancouver | tel. 604 9 80 38 00 | bluewater adventures.ca*

DAWSON CREEK

The Alaska Highway leads you into the wilderness of the Northern Rockies

Dawson Creek (pop. 12,000) would have been an inconspicuous farm-ing village had it not been for *Milestone 0* on the main road in the town centre. This is where the famous *Alaska Highway* begins.

Now fully paved, the road covers almost 2,300km to Delta Junction, Alaska. Exhibits in the *visitor centre* in the old station and the *Walter Wright* *Pioneer Village* illustrate the history of the region. The painstaking construc-tion of the highway by 30,000 American troops during World War II is illustrated in the *Alaska Highway House (Mon-Fri 9am-5pm | admission free | 10201 10th St).* ⟼ *H9*

ROCKY MOUNTAINS

BEARS & MOUNTAINS

The Rockies offer all of the clichés commonly associated with Canada: emerald glacial lakes, rugged peaks, colourful wild-flower meadows and grizzlies feasting on blueberries. It is not surprising that the mountains on the border between Alberta and British Columbia are the most famous and popular tourist region in Western Canada.

Five major national parks attract visitors; four of them – Banff, Jasper, Kootenay and Yoho – border each other and form a nature

The view from Sulphur Mountain in Banff National Park

reserve in the heart of the Rockies that covers 20,000km². Through its centre runs the Icefields Parkway, a legendary route along the backbone of the continent. In summer, large numbers of visitors descend on areas such as Banff, Jasper and Lake Louise, and hotels are usually fully booked. You are better off at campsites and at the edge of the parks, in places such as Canmore. However, it is still possible to enjoy the Rockies in glorious tranquillity: the parks have excellent hiking trails where you can be all on your own.

ROCKY MOUNTAINS

MARCO POLO HIGHLIGHTS

★ **ICEFIELDS PARKWAY**
The most spectacular scenic road in the Rockies: high passes with views of glaciers and emerald lakes ➤ p. 88

★ **FAIRMONT BANFF SPRINGS HOTEL**
Once a castle hotel for royalty and stars; today you can enjoy a drink on the terrace ➤ p. 88

★ **LAKE LOUISE**
Despite the crowds of tourists, it remains a uniquely beautiful lake ➤ p. 89

★ **KANANASKIS COUNTRY**
The recreational region on the sunny eastern mountain slopes of the Rockies is beautiful but not crowded ➤ p. 93

★ **TAKAKKAW FALLS**
The highest waterfalls in the Rocky Mountains – especially beautiful in the afternoon ➤ p. 98

★ **WATERTON SHORELINE CRUISES**
Idyllic boat trip, surrounded by mountains, on the US border ➤ p. 99

★ **FORT STEELE**
Perfectly restored gold rush town ➤ p. 101

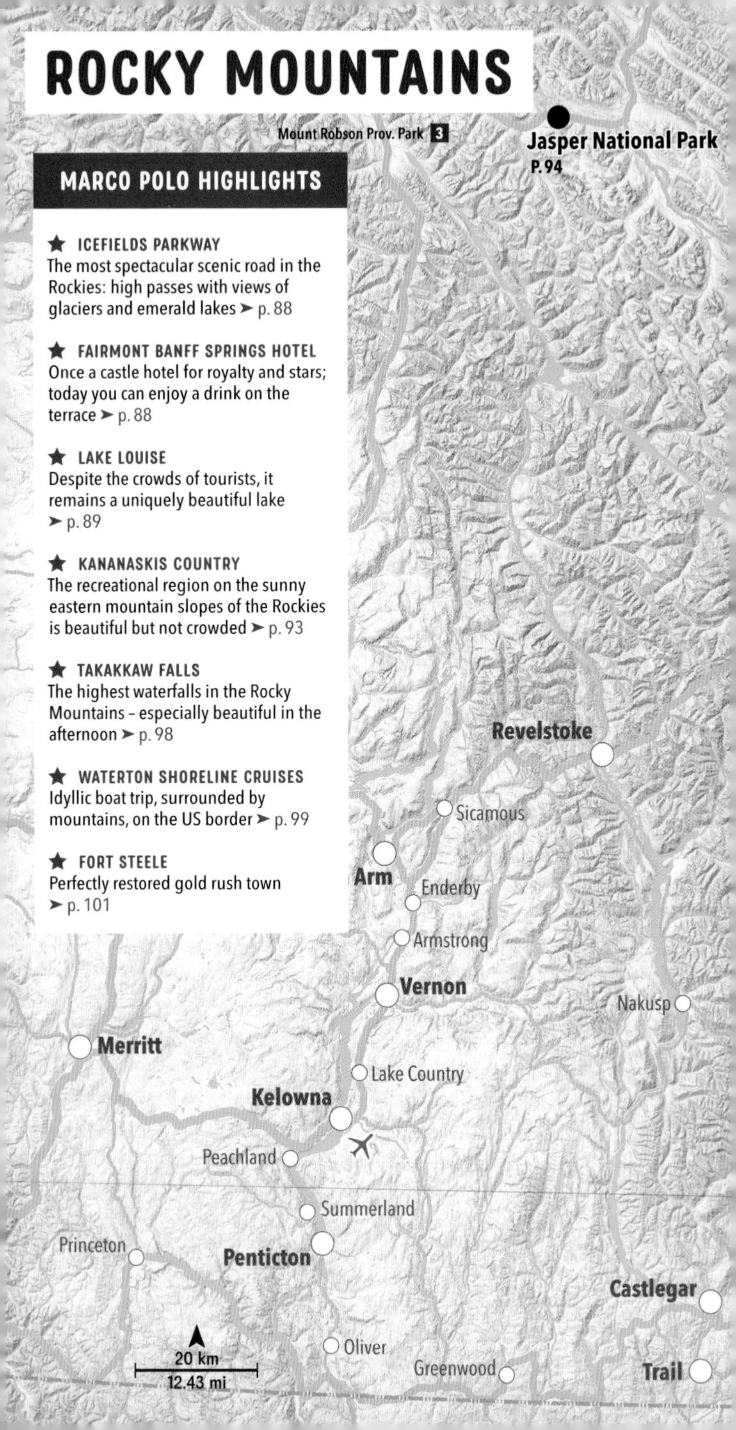
Mount Robson Prov. Park 3
Jasper National Park
P.94
Revelstoke
Sicamous
Arm
Enderby
Armstrong
Vernon
Nakusp
Merritt
Lake Country
Kelowna
Peachland
Summerland
Princeton
Penticton
Castlegar
Oliver
Greenwood
Trail
20 km
12.43 mi

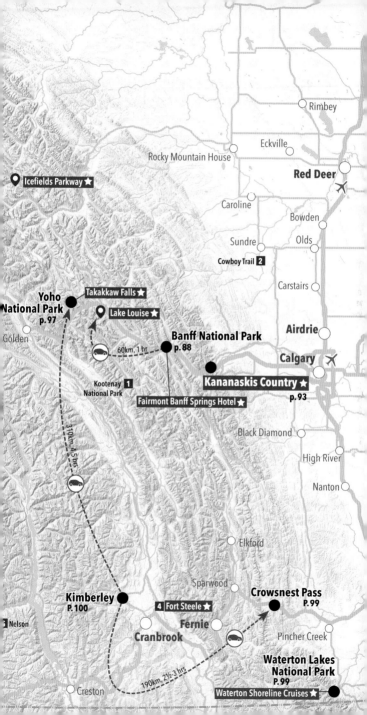

Rimbey

Eckville

Rocky Mountain House

Red Deer ✈

Caroline

Bowden

Olds

Sundre

Cowboy Trail **2**

Carstairs

Icefields Parkway ★

Takakkaw Falls ★

Yoho National Park p. 97

Lake Louise ★

Banff National Park p. 88

Airdrie

Golden

60km, 1 hr

Calgary ✈

Kootenay National Park **1**

Kananaskis Country ★ p. 93

Fairmont Banff Springs Hotel ★

310km, 4-5 hrs

Black Diamond

High River

Nanton

Elkford

Sparwood

Kimberley P. 100

4 Fort Steele ★

Crowsnest Pass P. 99

Nelson

Fernie

Cranbrook

Pincher Creek

Waterton Lakes National Park P. 99

190km, 2½-3 hrs

Creston

Waterton Shoreline Cruises ★

BANFF NAT. PARK

(☐ J12–13) **The oldest national park in Canada comprises 6,640km² of glacier valleys, emerald lakes and snow-capped mountain peaks in the Bow River valley.**

As early as 1885, when the railway was constructed in the region, the Canadian government decided to make the mountain landscape a nature reserve. Due to the strict regulations only a small part of the park was opened to the public, including the town of *Banff* (pop. 5,000) and a few ski areas. A cable car brings you to the top of *Sulphur Mountain* and to a vantage point overlooking the city and the Bow River. Some hotels were built along *Lake Louise*, but the mountain wilderness stretches around these oases of civilisation, just as it always has. In 2018, bison, which had become extinct in the pioneer era, were re-introduced to the park. *Park wardens* in the Banff or Lake Louise *visitor centres* have hiking maps for more than 1,300km of remote trails. For details please visit: *parkscanada.ca, banfflakelouise.com*

SIGHTSEEING

ICEFIELDS PARKWAY ★

"The most beautiful journey in the world" is the byline of the 230-km-long Hwy 93 from Lake Louise to Jasper. The road runs along the ridge of the mountains past ancient glaciers and alpine lakes, waterfalls and sweeping summits. It pays to start the journey early, because the best views are to the west, and the soft morning sun catches the rock walls and ice falls.

And keep your camera ready, because quite often you will spot the park's animals along the way: a Wapiti deer or moose, mountain sheep or goats – and with a bit of luck you may even see a grizzly. The most beautiful views await at ⚑ *Bow Pass* viewpoint (2,068m) with the remarkable milky-green of *Peyto Lake* and the canyons further up the valley. Other worthwhile stops include *Mistaya Canyon*, *Waterfowl Lake* (with a beautiful campsite) and the *Sunwapta Falls*.

WHYTE MUSEUM OF THE ROCKIES

Exhibits relate to the Rockies, the pioneer era and the first Swiss mountain guides. Guided tours to pioneer cabins are available. *Daily 10am–5pm | admission C$10 | 111 Bear St | Banff | ⏱ 1 hr*

FAIRMONT BANFF SPRINGS HOTEL ★

The ostentatious hotel above the Bow River was built in 1886 by the Canadian Pacific Railroad. The railway director William Cornelius Van Horne was the driving force behind the construction of this majestic castle hotel. His belief was, "If we cannot export the scenery, we must import the tourists", so, along with the Canadian Pacific Railroad (completed in 1885), he had a series of luxury hotels

The Icefields Parkway is one of the most impressive scenic roads in the world

constructed. The Banff Springs, which resembles a Scottish castle, is one of the most beautiful examples of these "railway hotels". Its terrace bar is perfect for enjoying a drink. *Spray Av. | Banff*

CAVE & BASIN NATIONAL HISTORIC SITE

Exhibitions on the park's history are housed in the old bath house of the hot springs – the park's origin – and all around you will find beautiful nature trails, including the *Marsh Trail (daily in summer 9am–5pm, otherwise 11am–5pm | admission C$4 | 311 Cave Av. | Banff)* with its many lookout points.

MOUNT NORQUAY

In winter, the 2,133-m-high peak above the village of Banff is a very popular ski resort. When you visit in summer, you should take the chairlift and enjoy the panoramic view from the *Cliffhouse Bistro*.

To get the adrenaline going, there are guided tours for beginners on a complex climbing route with rope bridges and steel ladders. *Daily 9am–7pm | chairlift C$35 | 2 Mount Norquay Rd | Banff | banffnorquay.com | ⏱ 2–6 hrs*

INSIDER TIP A peak experience

LAKE LOUISE ★

Canada's most famous lake shimmers in turquoise hues at the foot of the 3,464-m-high Mount Victoria. The waterfront at *Chateau Lake Louise* (another railway hotel) is a constant hustle and bustle, but you will find the paths around it much quieter. The trails, such as *Big Beehive/Lake Agnes Trail* or the *Plain of Six Glaciers Trail*, are ideal for a day's excursion. *Moraine Lake* in the *Valley of Ten Peaks*, 15km to the south, is another perfect location for a selfie. *Get there by shuttle bus from Lake Louise Village*

BUFFALO NATIONS LUXTON MUSEUM 🎭

Detailed, re-staged scenes from the daily life of the First Nations bring history alive and are not just entertaining for children. The museum features daily activities such as drumming, teepee-making or crafting feather headdresses. *Daily in summer 10am–7pm, otherwise 11am–5pm | admission C$10, children C$5 | 1 Birch Av. | Banff | ⟳ 2 hrs*

INSIDER TIP
A First Nation experience

ROCKIES HELI CANADA

Spectacular helicopter excursions over the Central Rockies and the Columbia Icefield. Starts on Hwy 11, 40km east of the Icefields Parkway. *Cline River | Hwy 11 | tel. 888 8 44 35 14 and 403 8 81 25 00 | rockiesheli.com*

EATING & DRINKING

COYOTE'S

Bistro with a creative, modern Mexican cuisine. Also gluten-free dishes and organic ingredients. Open all day. *206 Caribou St | Banff | tel. 403 7 62 39 63 | C$$*

JUNIPER BISTRO

Organic cuisine with regional ingredients and great views over Banff from the terrace or the bar. Slightly off the beaten track, at the edge of the town in the newly renovated *Juniper Hotel (C$$–$$$)*. *1 Juniper Way | Banff | tel. 403 7 63 62 19 | C$$–$$$*

LAKE LOUISE STATION RESTAURANT

A true classic: refined regional cuisine in an old Canadian Pacific railway station. *200 Sentinel Rd | Lake Louise | tel. 403 5 22 26 00 | C$$–$$$*

NUM-TI-JAH LODGE

A good place for a break on Icefields Parkway: historic lodge on the shores of Bow Lake. Traditional furnishings and a good restaurant. During the day, they serve an excellent bison chilli in the small café. *Icefields Parkway | 40km north of Lake Louise | tel. 403 5 22 21 67 | sntj.ca | C$$$*

SALTLIK

Chic restaurant with a large bar on the ground floor. Serves steaks and fresh fish daily. *221 Bear St | Banff | tel. 403 7 62 24 67 | C$$–$$$*

SUSHI HOUSE 🐟

Tiny but excellent, the sushi comes to the table on a model train. *304 Caribou St | Banff | tel. 403 7 62 43 53 | C$*

INSIDER TIP
The fish arrives by train

WILD FLOUR BAKERY

The bakery not only offers good bread made from organic ingredients but also soups, sandwiches and a great early breakfast for hikers. *Daily 7am–4pm | 211 Bear St | Banff | tel. 403 7 60 50 74 | C$*

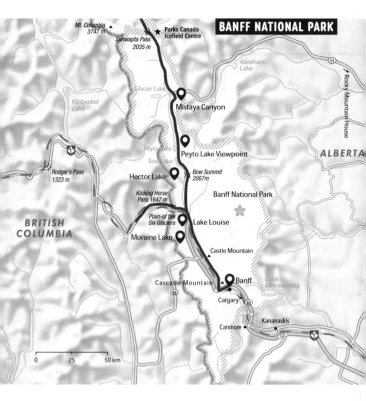

Map labels:
- Mt. Columbia 3747 m
- Sunwapta Pass 2035 m
- Parks Canada Icefield Centre
- **BANFF NATIONAL PARK**
- Abraham Lake
- Glacier Lake
- Kinbasket Lake
- Mistaya Canyon
- Peyto Lake
- Peyto Lake Viewpoint
- ALBERTA
- Rocky Mountain House
- Rodger's Pass 1323 m
- Bow Lake
- Hector Lake
- Bow Summit 2067 m
- Kicking Horse Pass 1647 m
- Banff National Park
- BRITISH COLUMBIA
- Plain of the Six Glaciers
- Lake Louise
- Moraine Lake
- Castle Mountain
- Banff
- Cascade Mountain
- Lake Minnewanka
- Calgary
- Canmore
- Kananaskis

0   25   50 km

SHOPPING

Banff Avenue is full of souvenir shops selling T-shirts, fleece jackets and sweet chocolate temptations. The shops in the side streets offer better quality and a greater range of products, for example the *Canada House Gallery (201 Bear St)*, that only sells arts and crafts that were actually produced in Canada.

SPORT & ACTIVITIES

ADVENTURES UNLIMITED

This is the place to arrange all kinds of activity tours in the national parks: be it horse riding, guided hiking tours or rafting trips. And in winter you can even do some dog sledding. *211 Bear St | Banff | tel. 403 762 45 54 | banffadventures.com*

BACTRAX BIKE RENTAL

Bike rental for day trips in and around Banff. Good tips for routes. *225 Bear St | tel. 403 762 81 77 | snowtips-bactrax.com*

HIKING

Outside of Banff you'll find some shorter hikes into the *Vermillion Lakes* area, such as the 1.5-km *Fenland Trail*. Wapiti deer, moose and beaver are often spotted on the trail, despite its proximity to the Trans-Canada Highway. A 2km trail from the parking lot of the Mount Norquay ski area leads to the summit of *Stoney Squaw Mountain*, with a breathtaking panoramic view over the Banff Valley and *Lake Minnewanka*.

Other great hiking destinations for day trips are *Spray River valley*, *Sunshine Meadows* and *Johnstone Canyon*. Also highly recommended are trails that begin at Lake Louise and nearby Moraine Lake, over the *Sentinel Pass* into *Paradise Valley* or to the *Wenkchemna Pass*.

WELLNESS

UPPER HOT SPRINGS
After your hike relax those muscles in a steaming bath. *Daily in summer 9am–11pm, otherwise 10am–10pm | admission C$8.30 | Mountain Av. | Banff | hotsprings.ca*

NIGHTLIFE

BANFF CENTRE 🍸
In July/August, this globally appraised music and art academy stages concerts and performances by predominantly young award-winning talent. Tickets: *banffcentre.ca*

WILD BILL'S LEGENDARY SALOON
Hearty Wild West food, live music, lots of wooden decor and plenty of beer make for an excellent atmosphere.

Nice balcony with a view of the action on Banff Avenue. *201 Banff Av. | Banff | tel. 403 7 62 03 33 | C$–$$*

AROUND BANFF

1 KOOTENAY NATIONAL PARK
50km / 35 mins by car from Banff to the Marble Canyon
The large, protected region with an area of 1,406km² around the valley of the Kootenay River is heavily infested by the bark beetle, but the hinterland is good for hiking tours. Various short trails lead from Hwy 93 (which runs through the park) such as one along the *Marble Canyon* and another to the orange and ochre *Paint Pots* where the First Nations got their pigments for making war paint.

When your muscles are sore from hiking, you can relax at the southern entrance to the park where hot water bubbles up (sometimes at hot as 47°C) at the *Radium Hot Springs (admission C$7.30 | hotsprings.ca)*, the largest (25m) mineral bathing pools in Canada.

If you like hiking far from civilisation and are interested in Native American wisdom, there's a good site at the southern edge of the park in the Kootenay River valley. The *Cross River Wilderness Centre (Settlers Rd | Radium Hot Springs | tel. 403 2 71 32 96 | crossriver.ca | C$$)*

INSIDER TIP
Log cabins in the wilderness

has eight solar-powered cabins and teepees.

KANANASKIS COUNTRY

(🗺 K13) **Banff may be more famous, but the recreational area of ⭐ 🐗 Kananaskis Country between Banff and Calgary, on the sunny eastern edge of the Rockies, is just as attractive – and it's free!**

Kanananaskis Country is noted for recreation and tourism. The majority of the valley is a nature reserve and offers excellent sports activities including a championship golf course as well as a vast network of hiking and cycling paths. The *Peter Lougheed Provincial Park* at the southern end of the valley, where the lakes are framed by 3,000-m-high peaks, is particularly popular. You can enjoy some very good hiking and some fantastic views on the trails around the *Highwood Pass* or to the *Ribbon Falls* and on the *Mount Indefatigable Trail*.

A landscape made for giants surrounds the Giant Steps waterfall in Paradise Valley

AROUND KANANASKIS COUNTRY

2 COWBOY TRAIL

Approx. 100km / 1 hr by car from Kananaski

Alongside Hwy 22 runs the *Cowboy Trail*, a panoramic drive through ranch country in the foothills of the Rockies. For information about riding, ranches and restaurants you can visit *the cowboytrail.com*. Worth seeing is the ✈ *Bar U Ranch* (daily 10am–5pm), near *Longview*, a National Historic Site and original 1882 ranch that

60 MILLION YEARS OLD

The Rockies are the easternmost string of the North American Cordilleras. In Canada, this mighty mountain range is 1,200km long and it ends far to the north in the Yukon Territory. The ranges are composed of sedimentary rock, slate, limestone and sandstone which were deposited on the seabed of a primeval ocean during prehistory. About 60 million years ago, the range was pushed up by movements in the earth's crust. Over time, ice-age glaciers carved today's valleys, leaving behind turquoise melt-water lakes and vast moraines. These are now being enjoyed by naturalists and wilderness adventurers alike.

preserves Alberta's cowboy history. Horse-drawn carriage rides and exhibitions are also on offer. ⌐ *K12–13*

JASPER NAT. PARK

(⌐ *H–J 11–12*) **On the roof of the continent: the 10,800-km² park at the northern edge of the Icefields Parkway is famous for its glaciers and less crowded than Banff.**

You absolutely must see the idyllic *Maligne Lake* and take a relaxing soak in the hot springs of *Miette*. Accommodation and restaurants can be found in *Jasper*, the only village within the park. The *visitor centre* is opposite the railway station.

ATHABASCA GLACIER

The glacier is part of the 215-km² *Columbia Icefield*, a remnant from the last ice age whose melt water runs into three oceans: the Atlantic, Pacific and Arctic. As recently as 100 years ago, ice filled the entire valley where Hwy 93 is today. Signs on the roadside indicate just how fast the glacier is retreating.

The tours offered to the glacier in specially adapted vehicles are a bit touristy. You may prefer to go on your own or take a guided hike with *Ice Walk* (icewalks.com). Otherwise, hike across the glacier on the Parker Ridge Trail further south, which offers great views. And if you're after a thrill, you can visit the *Glacier Discovery Skywalk* *(daily in summer 9am–6pm | admission C$99 | ⏱ 3–4 hrs)* and stroll across a glass platform suspended 300m above the valley of the Sunwapta River.

JASPER SKYTRAM

Cable car to *Whistler Mountain* offering magnificent panoramic views over the valley of Jasper. There are walking

views. Restaurant/shop at the first bridge. *Maligne Lake Rd, approx. 20km east of Jasper*

MALIGNE LAKE BOAT TOURS

Ninety-minute cruises on the largest glacier lake in the Rocky Mountains including the famous *Spirit Island*. The best time is in the late afternoon. *Daily in summer every half-hour*

The Glacier Discovery Walk high above the valley is simply spectacular

paths around the summit. *Daily in summer 8am–9pm, otherwise 10am–5pm | ticket C$47 | Whistler Rd | Jasper*

MALIGNE CANYON

Various bridges, steep steps and trails provide access to an incredible gorge with a 50-m drop to the Maligne River which makes its thunderous way through the rocks. There are routes of different lengths offering fantastic

8.30am–5.30pm | ticket C$79, book in Jasper | 616 Patricia St | tel. 780 8 52 33 70

SPORT & ACTIVITIES

SKYLINE TRAIL RIDES

Half-day horse rides, but also three-day trail rides with overnight stay in a wilderness lodge. Book in advance. *Tel. 780 8 52 42 15 | skylinetrail.com*

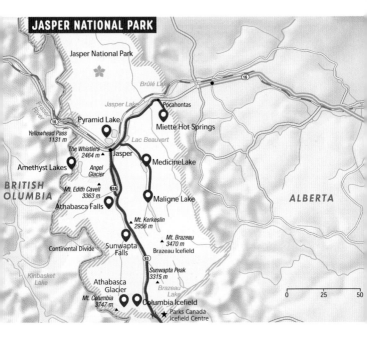

HIKING

The most beautiful and most popular short trails are at the foot of *Mount Edith Cavell* and at *Maligne Canyon*. Especially suitable for day hikes and longer trips are the *Tonquin Valley* and the wilderness region of *Brazeau Lake*. Black bears are everywhere in Jasper National Park: they curiously investigate campsites and sometimes stroll at leisure on the highway. In contrast, you will only encounter the rather shy grizzlies deeper in the Rocky Mountains, although in spring they can also be seen alongside the highways in Jasper. Please be aware that these are wild animals and you always need to proceed with caution: keep your distance when taking pictures, and if you're camping, store all food in the car overnight and make sure you wash up any plates that smell of steak.

EATING & DRINKING

DOWNSTREAM RESTAURANT

Venison steaks, salmon and bison ribs in a refined atmosphere. *620 Connaught Dr. | Jasper | tel. 780 8 52 94 49 | C$$–$$$*

PAPA GEORGE'S

If you are really hungry, try this cosy bar in the Astoria Hotel serving steaks and fish dishes. They also do an excellent big breakfast. *404 Connaught Dr. | Jasper | tel. 780 8 52 22 60 | C$$*

TEKARRA LODGE

Rustic and historic log cabins with fire-places. Also a good restaurant serving regional specialities such as moose carpaccio or bison ribs. *Hwy 93A S | tel. 780 8 52 46 24 | tekarralodge.com | C$$–$$$*

SIDER TIP
By the wild Athabasca River

AROUND JASPER

3 MOUNT ROBSON PROV. PARK

90km / 1 hr by car from Jasper

To the west of Jasper is the highest peak in the Canadian Rockies, the 3,954-m summit of Mount Robson. In good weather, the mountain is visible from the *visitor centre* on Hwy 16. A recommended one- to two-day hike takes you along the Robson River at the foot of the ice-covered range to the Berg Lake. *H12*

YOHO NAT. PARK

(K13) **This park is located in the valleys of the Kicking Horse and Yoho rivers on the western slopes of the Rocky Mountains. It is "a mere" 1,313km² and is not nearly as well known as its big brother, the Banff National Park.**

This has its advantages as it is far quieter, but no less spectacular, with stunning nature and beautiful mountain scenery, including the second highest waterfalls in Canada. You can

The Rocky Mountain goat is the iconic animal of Mount Robson

The name says it all: the striking Emerald Lake

easily explore the Yoho National Park on a day trip from Lake Louise or Banff.

SIGHTSEEING

TAKAKKAW FALLS ★

The 344m-high Takakkaw Falls, fed by melt water from the *Wapta Icefield*, are a magnificent spectacle of nature. The falls, around 5km north of Field, are the second high-est in Canada. In the afternoon, when the midday sun melts the glacial ice, the cas-cades are at their most impressive.

INSIDER TIP
Sparkling melt water

KICKING HORSE PASS

The Trans-Canada Highway traverses the national park and climbs up to the Kicking Horse Pass (1,647m) over the watershed between the Pacific and the Arctic Ocean. To cope with the large differences in height, the rail-way engineers drilled two spiral tunnels into the mountain some 100 years ago. If you get lucky, you can watch freight trains with more than 100 box wagons exiting the upper part of the tunnel while the last wagons are still entering – it's a curious sight.

EMERALD LAKE

The ultimate Rockies sensation: a surfaced hiking path that leads round the shimmering, emerald-green and turquoise lake, surrounding the mountain glacier slopes that reach up to an altitude of over 3,000m. In summer, a 🛶 canoe tour is a beauti-ful experience (book at the lake).

EATING & DRINKING

TRUFFLE PIGS

Regional organic cuisine in the national park's only village. Having tried the BBQ duck or salmon with tabbouleh, make sure you still have space for the delicious desserts. They also run a small hotel. *12 rooms | 100 Centre St | Field | tel. 250 3 43 63 03 | trufflepigs.com | C$$*

Hwy 22 | Lundbreck | tel. 403 6 28 24 31 | sierrawestcabins.com | C$$

CROWSNEST PASS

(□ K14) **The Crowsnest Pass is the southernmost pass over the Canadian Rockies. It was once an important First Nation trading route. Today, the modern Hwy 3 crosses through the densely forested mountains at a height of 1,396m.**

The Crowsnest Pass has a series of small towns – such as *Bellevue*, *Frank* and *Coleman* – located along the highway. They were all established as mining towns around 1900. Frank is infamous for a horrendous landslide in 1903 that buried the village and killed 90 people. An excellent museum, the *Frank Slide Interpretive Centre (daily in summer 9am–6pm, otherwise 10am–5pm | admission C$13)*, shows the history of coal mining in the region, the avalanche and also has a trail that winds through the rocks of *Frank Slide*.

SPORT & ACTIVITIES

SIERRA WEST RANCH

The cowboy lifestyle: this traditional ranch in the foothills of the Rockies has log cabins, saloon and daily riding. In the summer you can participate in one of several cattle drives. *6 cabins |*

WATERTON LAKES NAT. PARK

(□ K14–15) **The 525-km² park on the edge of the prairies was named after the series of lakes that stretch far south across the border to the Glacier National Park in Montana, USA.**

At *Cameron Lake* you can hire boats and canoes, and at the northern edge of the park you can observe a small herd of bison in an enclosure. The best views of the lake and mountains are from the terrace of the *Prince of Wales Hotel* at the northern edge of *Waterton Park*, the only village in the reserve.

Good hiking trails lead into the hinterland which is still pristine. A particularly beautiful short trail goes to the *Red Rock Canyon*, whose fiery red walls are made up of 1.5 billion-year-old sediment stone.

SIGHTSEEING

WATERTON SHORELINE CRUISES ★

The company offers boat trips on the *Upper Waterton Lake*. The southernmost point of the cruise is in the *Glacier National Park* in Montana, USA. The views of the majestic mountains are especially good in the early morning. There is also a ferry service for hikers. *Departure from the Waterton marina daily in summer 10am, 1pm, 4pm, 7pm | ticket C$51 | tel. 403 8 59 23 62 | watertoncruise.com*

SPORT & ACTIVITIES

CRYPT LAKE HIKE

INSIDER TIP
A crazy hike The most unusual day hike in the Canadian Rockies costs you only C$26 or the price of a ferry ride across Waterton Lake. The trail runs steeply uphill on the other shore. In the end you have to climb up a ladder and through a tunnel to *Crypt Lake* high up in the mountains. *Departures daily in summer 8.30am, 9am and 10am | Waterton Townsite*

KIMBERLEY

(🗺 J14) **This town (pop. 6,600) on the western edge of the Rocky Mountains is known as the "Bavarian City of the Rockies".**

When the local mine closed in 1972 and it seemed that Kimberley would become a ghost town, the city fathers decided to turn it into a Bavarian village, and it worked: the mountain scenery is the ideal backdrop and the architecture is now thoroughly alpine. The shops on the pedestrian *platzl* sell Bavarian knick-knacks; there is an oversized cuckoo clock; and in the restaurants the bands play traditional German music. Even the fire hydrants are painted with *lederhosen* and *dirndl*.

Nina's Hillside Garden View (440 Spokane St | tel. 250 4 27 46 81 | C$$)

Are we really in Canada? A Bavarian restaurant in Kimberley

serves tasty sandwiches and home-made soup in a garden that has a miniature Swiss village and carvings. At *Kootenay Rockies Tourism (1905 Warren Av. | tel. 250 4 27 48 38 | kootenayrockies.com)* you can get information on accommodation, ranches, golf courses and hiking trails.

AROUND KIMBERLEY

4 FORT STEELE ★

40km / 30 mins by car from Kimberley

East of Kimberley, in the valley of the young Columbia River, the gold rush era is brought to life in the Fort Steele heritage town. It was founded in 1865 as a post for the Northwest Mounted Police and became the largest settlement in the region – although it was soon forgotten after the gold rush. Today it lives on as a museum town and more than 60 buildings have been restored or moved here from the surrounding area. Costumed actors enact the life of the pioneers and a stagecoach runs through the village *(performances daily in summer 10am–5pm | admission C$17).*

Accommodation is in a historic boarding school and mission and there's a championship golf course run by a First Nation community: the St Eugene Resort *(125 rooms | 7777 Mission Rd |*

INSIDER TIP
A dream backdrop for golfers

Cranbrook | tel. 250 4 20 20 00 | steugene.ca | C$$)* ⌁ *J14*

5 NELSON

250km / 3 hrs by car west of Kimberley

Nelson (pop. 10,000), the oldest town in the Kootenay region, oozes Victorian charm. The courthouse with tower and turret, the magnificent bank made of Kootenay marble and the Wild West shop façades document its elegant past as a rich mining town. Today, thanks to an alternative young scene and the superb conditions for mountain biking and hiking in the provincial parks, the town is thriving. In August, red salmon spawn in Kootenay Creek on the edge of town. ⌁ *J130*

WHERE TO STAY IN THE ROCKY MOUNTAINS

CANADIAN IDYLL

A place to relax and slow down with well-maintained log cabins and a bubbling brook, a 15-minute drive from Lake Louise. *Baker Creek Chalets (33 rooms | Hwy. 1A | Lake Louise | tel. 403 5 22 37 61 | baker creek.com | C$$$).*

IN THE HEART OF THE ROCKIES

Secluded in a high valley, this rustic mountain inn serves great food and is perfectly situated for hikers. Also open in winter. *Mount Engadine Lodge (6 rooms and 3 cabins | Canmore | tel. 403 6 78 40 80 | mountengadine.com | incl. full board | C$$)*

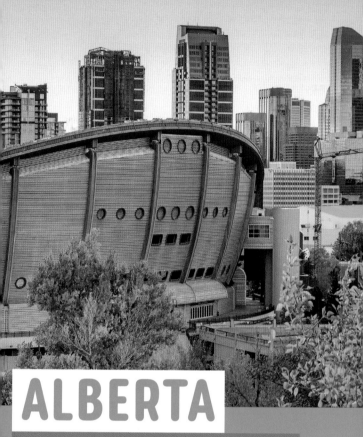

ALBERTA

PRAIRIES STRETCHING TO THE HORIZON

The Rocky Mountains are the most famous region of Alberta, but they only make up a small part of the vast 661,200-km² province. East of the Rockies, the endless prairies of Central Canada stretch up into the vast subarctic forests of the north.

Alberta is above all a land of farmers and ranchers interspersed with small, sleepy villages. However, cowboy nostalgia does not reign throughout the province. In 1914, the first oil well gushed in Turner Valley near Calgary; in 1947 further large oil deposits were

The skyline of Calgary

discovered near Edmonton. Since then, the two major cities have boomed, and the oil-rich province provides close to 80 per cent of Canada's fossil energy resources.

The Mesozoic era provided the province not only with oil and coal: at that time dinosaurs lived on the edge of a prehistoric lake and their fossilised bones appear all over the sediment layers in south-ern Alberta. In fact, the province is the largest dinosaur graveyard in the world.

ALBERTA

Mayerthorpe

Edson

Hinton

Drayton Valley

Jasper

300km 3 hrs

Eckville

Rocky Mountain House

MARCO POLO HIGHLIGHTS

★ **CALGARY STAMPEDE**
Cowboys from all over the world take part in the planet's biggest rodeo in early July ➤ p. 106

★ **RANCHMAN'S SALOON**
Steaks, line dancing and country music – what more does a wannabe cowboy need? The Wild West is alive and kicking here! ➤ p. 110

★ **ROYAL TYRRELL MUSEUM**
In Drumheller the museum displays massive dinosaurs in a primeval landscape; new fossils are continuously being discovered in the sandstone ➤ p. 111

★ **HEAD-SMASHED-IN BUFFALO JUMP**
Where the Blackfoot Nation once drove herds of bison over the cliff, today their story is being told ➤ p. 112

★ **WEST EDMONTON MALL**
The biggest shopping centre in Canada, including fun in the wave pool, crazy golf at night and Columbus's caravel ➤ p. 116

Caroline

Sundre

Banff

Cochrane

Canmore

Elkford

Kimberley

Sparwood

Cranbrook

Fernie

Castlegar

Trail

Creston

Newgate

CALGARY

(🔲 K13) **Skyscrapers, boutiques, sidewalk cafés and urban sculptures – Calgary (pop. 1.5 million) is a thriving metropolis.**

Stroll through the Stephen Avenue Mall. It's like a proud Manhattan in the prairie. There's reason enough for all the extravagance: the oil boom of recent decades rapidly made Calgary the fourth-largest city in Canada.

Calgary's history starts in 1875 when a police post along the Bow River was installed to combat illegal whiskey trading. The Trans-Canada Railway was built in 1883; soon after, the first ranches were established and Calgary became the capital of Canada's meat industry. The discovery of oil in Turner Valley in 1914 triggered the first oil boom, and Calgary took off. In 1988 the city hosted the Olympic Winter Games, putting it firmly on the international map. Despite the industrial boom, the city likes to maintain its cowboy image and every July, for the past century, has hosted the largest rodeo in the world, the ★ *Calgary Stampede*.

SIGHTSEEING

CALGARY TOWER

On a clear day the panoramic view from this 191m-tall tower (with a revolving restaurant) is incredible. *Daily in summer 9am–10pm, otherwise until 9pm | admission C\$18 | 9th Av./Centre St | 🔲 j4*

CITY CENTRE

Walk from Calgary Tower through the city centre via the pedestrian area on 8th Avenue to the *Olympic Plaza* where the medals of the 1988 winter games were awarded. 🐷 Today, the well-known square becomes busy at lunch time, featuring free concerts, street artists and food stalls. Just north on Centre Street is *Chinatown* and the *Chinese Cultural Centre (197 1st St)*. East of that, on the banks of the Bow River, are the foundations of the Fort Calgary police post, which today houses a visitor centre. *🔲 j–k2–4*

GLENBOW MUSEUM

The history of the Native Americans and settlers in Western Canada is documented on three floors of exhibits. *Mon–Sat 9am–5pm, Sun noon–5pm; in winter closed on Mon | admission C\$16 | 130 9th Av. SE | ⏱ 2 hrs | 🔲 j4*

STUDIO BELL

A recording studio with a cool design, which is also the National Music

---

WHERE TO START?

Calgary Tower, at 101 9th Av. (park on 9th Av. one block to the east), makes an excellent starting point. Opposite the tower is the Glenbow Museum. The Stephen Avenue Mall pedestrian zone is one street to the north. Turning left, you get to the business district, while on the right is the Olympic Plaza, constructed for the 1988 winter games.

The Calgary Stampede is the world's biggest rodeo show with 1.5 million visitors

Centre celebrating many of Canada's artists – from country stars to the Barenaked Ladies. Concerts are held almost daily, and you are often welcome to come and discover new music. *Wed–Sun 10am–5pm | admission C$18 | 850 4th St SE | ⊙ 2 hrs | ▥ k4*

PEACE BRIDGE

An architectural highlight: the Spanish architect Santiago Calatrava built this glazed steel bridge in 2012 for the increasing numbers of pedestrians and cyclists crossing the Bow River. It is especially attractive when illuminated at night when it is beautifully illuminated. *7th St SW/1st Av. SW*

CALGARY ZOO & PREHISTORIC PARK

A zoo where Siberian tigers, pandas as well as many of the typical animals of Canada are kept in big, natural enclosures. A special attraction is a "Jurassic Park" with life-size dinosaurs. *Daily 9am–5pm | admission C$35, children C$25 | 1300 Zoo Rd NE | Calgary | calgaryzoo.org*

CANADA OLYMPIC PARK

The old Olympic centre's *Sports Hall of Fame (daily in summer 10am–5pm, otherwise closed Mon/Tue | admission C$12)* on the western edge of the city exhibits everything about sport in Canada. In summer there is ample opportunity to get your own adrenaline rush: on a zip line over the ski jump; on a free fall; on mountain biking trails; and on bobsleigh rides. *Activities from end June–early Oct | ticket C$20–190 | 88 Canada Olympic Rd | winsport.ca*

HERITAGE PARK HISTORICAL VILLAGE 👥

The extensive open-air museum on the shores of the Glenmore Reservoir depicts life in the Canadian Wild West and features a Native American camp, a fur trader fort, a reconstructed pioneer village, a steam train and paddle steamer. *Daily in summer 10am–5pm; in spring and autumn Sat/Sun only | admission C$26.25, children C$19 | 1900 Heritage Dr. SW | heritagepark. ca | ⏱ 3 hrs*

Shopping underneath tree sculptures on Stephen Avenue

EATING & DRINKING

MODEL MILK

A fashionable restaurant in an old dairy in the trendy 17th Avenue quarter. Modern Canadian cuisine is served tapas-style: bison tartar, halibut or calamari fricassée. *308 17th Av. SW | tel. 403 2 65 73 43 | C$$–$$$ | ⑩ h6*

MURRIETA'S

This is an excellent steakhouse in a historic building with traditional wood decor. The fish is excellent too. *808 1st St SW | tel. 403 2 69 77 07 | C$$$ | ⑩ j4*

THE NASH

A restaurant as hip as the city's Inglewood quarter where it's based. Located in a renovated historic hotel, The Nash serves fine Canadian cuisine with meat from the wood grill. There are numerous other bars and trendy restaurants in the vicinity. *925 11th St SE | tel. 403 9 84 33 65 | C$$–$$$*

ORIGINAL JOE'S

Small terrace in the pedestrian zone serving delicious burgers, tacos, salads and *poutine*. Also vegetarian dishes. *109 8th Av. SW | tel. 403 2 62 72 48 | C$ | ⑩ j4*

THE PALOMINO

This is a rustic BBQ restaurant and bar that serves hearty Tex-Mex

INSIDER TIP
24-hour BBQ

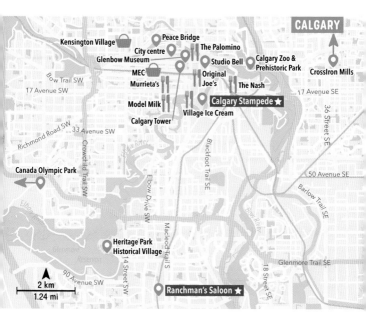

cuisine. In the evening they often have live rock or country music in the basement. *109 7th Av. SW | tel. 403 5 32 19 11 | C$-$$ | ⌖ j3*

VILLAGE ICE CREAM

Somewhat hidden on the eastern edge of the city centre, this is the best ice cream in town, as evidenced by the long queue outside. *431 10th Av. SE | C$ | ⌖ k4*

SHOPPING

Western clothes, cowboy boots and Stetsons are without doubt the most popular souvenirs from Calgary. You will find the best selection of outrageously decorated boots in brown, white, pink and any other colour imaginable at *Alberta Boot (50 50th Av. SE)*

and *Lammle's Western Wear* in the *Heritage Store (221 8th Av. SW)* by the *Stephen Avenue Mall*. There are many shopping malls along this avenue.

CROSSIRON MILLS 👕

Huge shopping centre on the northern edge of Calgary with approximately 200 stores and frequent sales. *Daily 10am-9pm, Sun until 6pm | 261055 Crossiron Blvd, Hwy 2 north of the airport | crossironmills.com*

KENSINGTON VILLAGE

Individual boutiques and galleries, alternative coffee shops and good pubs: take a stroll through the historical district along Kensington Road on the north side of the Bow River and see Calgary at its very best. *visit kensingtonyyc.com*

MEC

Everything is sustainable and eco-friendly at this sports shop in the west of the city centre. You will find quality equipment – ranging from tents to canoe paddles – for a tour in the wilds of Canada. *830 10 Av. SW | mec.ca*

SPORT & ACTIVITIES

SHAW MILLENNIUM PARK

The world's largest skatepark is located at the western end of the city centre. Almost 2 acres of pipes, stairs, jumps and ramps that are open to the public around the clock. *1220 9th Av. SW*

HUDSON'S BAY COMPANY

The development of Canada was largely thanks to the beaver and to European hat fashion. In the 17th and 18th centuries, hats made of Canadian beaver felt – especially tricornes and top hats – were all the rage. The woolly pelts of the large rodents were extremely profitable and, as a result, trappers and fur traders moved further and further west across the new continent. The Hudson's Bay Company, a fur company founded in 1670, became one of the world's biggest trading empires and their area of influence eventually covered one-twelfth of the earth's surface. Over time, the company's forts became cities and its trading routes developed into today's highways. Almost every Canadian town now has a 'Hudson's Bay' department store.

NIGHTLIFE

Many bars, restaurants and dance clubs are located along 17th Avenue SW between 4th and 8th Street. All country and western music fans should visit the ★ 👕 *Ranchman's Saloon (9615 Macleod Trail S)* where – according to the saloon's advertising – all the real cowboys meet (live music on Fridays, starting at 7pm, free 🐷 two-step and line-dancing lessons).

If you don't want to drive very far, then you should check out the *Knoxville's Tavern (840 9th Av. SW)* on the outskirts of the city centre. This is a popular dance club with live and country music evenings. Many live music pubs such as the *Ship and Anchor (534 17th Av. SW)* or the *Cafe Koi (1011 1st St SW)*, that also serves Asian-inspired cuisine, are located in the hip quarters on the south side of the city around *11th* and *17th Av.*

AROUND CALGARY

1 BLACKFOOT CROSSING HISTORICAL PARK

130km / 1.5 hrs by car from Calgary

In the middle of the prairies east of Calgary is the spectacular, newly built and eco-friendly cultural centre of the Blackfoot First Nation. Performances and exhibitions include dances, archaeological excavations, guided tours and teepee accommodation in

The Royal Tyrrell Museum in Drumheller is a must-visit for dinosaur fans

INSIDER TIP
A night in a teepee

an authentically reconstructed Native American village. The location of the cultural centre is significant: this was where the First Nations signed the treaty surrendering their land to Canadian government in 1877. *Daily in summer 9am–5pm | admission C$12 | Hwy 842 | Siksika | blackfoot-crossing.ca | ΩΩ K13*

2 DRUMHELLER

140km / 2 hrs by car from Calgary
North-east of Calgary by the Red Deer River are the *Alberta Badlands* – a bizarre barren landscape weathered by erosion. A drive along the 54-km *Dinosaur Trail* shows multi-coloured alluvial fans of deposits and strange rock pillars where many fossils have been discovered.

The most impressive finds of the dinosaurs that inhabited this region some 65 million years ago, when it had a tropical climate and lush vegetation, are housed in the ★ ⛺ 🦕 *Royal Tyrrell Museum (daily in summer 9am–9pm, otherwise Tue–Sun 10am–5pm | admission C$19, children C$10 | tyrrellmuseum.com | ⏱ 2–3 hrs).* The exhibits bring prehistory to life and include well-known species like Tyrannosaurus Rex and lesser-known dinosaurs with webbed feet. In summer, the museum's guides will show you how to look for fossils in the vicinity. *traveldrumheller.com | ΩΩ L13*

Shaped by the weather: the "Hoodos" in Writing-on-Stone Provincial Park

FORT MACLEOD

(□ K–L14) Fertile land on the banks of the Oldman River and with the Rockies on the horizon – it's no wonder the early settlers chose this site for their farming settlement (pop. 3,000).

SIGHTSEEING

THE FORT MUSEUM OF THE NORTH WEST MOUNTED POLICE

As early as 1874, the *Northwest Mounted Police* founded a fort to curb the whiskey trade with the First Nations – the first colonial outpost in the Wild West. In the (reconstructed) police fort, students give riding demonstrations in the historical uniforms of the Canadian police. Horse lovers may help staff groom the beautiful animals. *Daily in summer 9am–5pm | admission C$15 | Av. 219 Jerry Potts Blvd | nwmpmuseum.com*

INSIDER TIP
Assistant Mounties wanted

HEAD-SMASHED-IN BUFFALO JUMP ★ 🎭

A name can say it all: this is where the First Nations drove herds of bison over a cliff. The women waited below the cliff to cut up the animals and dry the meat for the winter provisions. The excellent museum about 20km west of Fort Macleod in the Blackfoot reservation details the lifestyle and hunting methods of the Plains First Nations. *Daily in summer 9am–5pm, otherwise 10am–5pm | admission C$15, children C$10 | Hwy 785 | headsmashedin.ca*

LETHBRIDGE

(￼ L14) **Once upon a time there were wild times in what is today the most important town (pop. 100,000) in the south of Alberta.**

In the *Indian Battle Park* on the western edge of the city is the notorious pioneer trading post *Fort Whoop-up*, where American whiskey traders cheated the Native Americans by trading highly overpriced whiskey for their furs *(May–Sept daily 10am–5pm, Thu until 9pm | admission C$10)*. Somewhat out of place in the prairie, albeit interesting, is the *Nikko Yuko Japanese Gardens* in Henderson Park, a manicured park in the traditional Japanese style *(May–June 10am–6pm; July/Aug 10am–7pm | admission C$11)*.

SIGHTSEEING

ALBERTA BIRDS OF PREY CENTRE 🐵

A sanctuary for birds of prey where injured falcons, owls and eagles are nursed back to health. Flying demonstrations every 90 minutes. *Daily in summer 9.30am–5pm | admission C$12, children C$8 | Coaldale/ Lethbridge | burrowingowl.com*

AROUND LETHBRIDGE

3 WRITING-ON-STONE PROVINCIAL PARK

90km / 1 hr by car from Lethbridge

The main attraction of the park in the steep Milk River valley, south of Lethbridge, are the hoodoos. These are oddly shaped stone pillars carved by wind and weather. The region was sacred to the Prairie First Nations who left behind many petroglyphs. *Guided tours daily in summer | tel. 403 6 47 23 64 to book | ￼ L14*

MEDICINE HAT

(￼ M14) **The biggest city in south-eastern Alberta (pop. 60,000) depends largely on the gas industry. It is a major stop on the Trans-Canada Highway and a supply centre for the farms in the surrounding district.**

The name "Medicine Hat" – a strange-sounding name for a town – probably originated during a time of conflict between the Blackfoot and Cree First Nations. A medicine man of the Cree lost his headdress in battle. This was interpreted as a bad omen by his community and it resulted in a bloody defeat.

AROUND MEDICINE HAT

4 CYPRESS HILLS PROVINCIAL PARK

80km / 1 hr by car from Medicine Hat

The Cypress Hills – the highest point in the prairie south-east of Medicine Hat – form a green oasis on the plains. During the last ice age, the region was not covered by glaciers, and as a result, this vegetation, which is atypical of the prairies, was able to establish itself. In *Loch Leven* you can hire canoes and bicycles. ⫿ *M14*

5 DINOSAUR PROVINCIAL PARK 👫

180km / 2 hrs by car from Medicine Hat

The bed of the Red Deer River, north-west of Medicine Hat, is one of the best dinosaur fossil sites in the world. Thirty-five species of dinosaur have already been discovered here, and the UNESCO has declared the region a World Heritage Site. There are nature trails and bus tours to the archaeological sites and the *visitor centre* exhibits a selection of the finds. Fossil enthusiasts who want to stay overnight will enjoy *Comfort Camping (7 tents | May–Oct tel. 877 5 37 27 57 | albertaparks. ca/dinosaur.aspx | C$–$$)* on the banks of the Red Deer River, where all the equipment – including comfortable beds – is included. ⫿ *L13*

EDMONTON

(⫿ K–L11) **From the fur-trading era to the gold rush and the oil boom – the provincial capital of Alberta has developed from a small village to a metropolis of 1.4 million inhabitants.**

The government and oil industry are the main employers although there is little sign of the oil industry in the city itself. Its straight streets, neatly laid out in checkerboard style, criss-cross manicured neighbourhoods, while glass-and-steel office towers are springing up in the city centre. From a tourist's perspective, Edmonton, with its international airport, is mainly a springboard for trips to the Rockies and – via the Alaska Highway and Mackenzie Highway – to the far north of Canada.

SIGHTSEEING

CITY CENTRE

The modern city centre is located on a hill that overlooks the scenic valley of the North Saskatchewan River, which is fringed by numerous large parks. All the action takes place around the vibrant *Sir Winston Churchill Square* with its art galleries and theatres, while the main shopping street is *Jasper Avenue*.

ART GALLERY OF ALBERTA

From the outside it's clearly recognizable: it's all about the art. Inside there are over 6,000 historical and modern works by Canadian and international artists. *Tue/Wed 11am–8pm, Thu/Fri 11am–5pm, Sat/Sun 10am–5pm | admission C\$12.50 | 2 Sir Winston Churchill Square | youraga.ca*

ROYAL ALBERTA MUSEUM

After several years of restauration work, the largest museum in West Canada re-opened in 2018, showcasing the history of the pioneers as well as the culture of the indigenous peoples, 🐛 exciting dinosaurs and the world of (live) beetles and spiders. *Daily 9am–5pm | 9810 103a Av. NW | royalalbertamuseum.ca | ⏱ 2–3 hrs*

FORT EDMONTON PARK

The extensive open-air museum depicts the city's history from its fur-trading days up to the 21st century. The primitive dwellings of the Hudson Bay Company's fort, built in 1845, have been reconstructed in detail. *Daily in summer 10am–5pm | admission C\$26.50 | 7000 143rd St | fortedmontonpark.ca | ⏱ 2–3 hrs*

MUTTART CONSERVATORY

The beautiful botanical garden on the riverbank with four futuristic glass pyramids – each a different ecosystem – that look impressive against the urban skyline of the city centre. *Daily 10am–5pm, Wed/Thu until 9pm | admission C\$12.50 | 9626 96A St*

EATING & DRINKING

PACKRAT LOUIE

Chic bistro in the Old Strathcona district with creative new Canadian cuisine and superb pizza. *10335 83 Av. | tel. 780 4 33 01 23 | packratlouie. com | C\$\$\$*

The daringly curved façade of the Art Gallery of Alberta

SABOR
Excellent fish restaurant in the city centre featuring Portuguese-Canadian cuisine and a popular bar. *10220 103rd St | tel. 780 7 57 11 14 | C$$*

SHOPPING

WEST EDMONTON MALL ★
In the sixth largest shopping mall in the world you will find more than 800 shops and restaurants, a large  amusement park with a rollercoaster and rope course, an artificial lake (with submarines!) and even a wave pool, including a surf wave – all under one roof. *87th Av./170th St | wem.ca*

NIGHTLIFE

Night owls will love the university district of *Old Strathcona* on the south bank of the Saskatchewan. Around *82nd Avenue* (called *Whyte Avenue*) are numerous cafés, restaurants and music venues. Country and western music fans should head for the Cook *County Saloon (8010 103rd St),* while jazz lovers will enjoy live bands in the *Yardbird Suite (102nd St/86th Av.).*

AROUND EDMONTON

6 ELK ISLAND NATIONAL PARK
40km / 30 mins by car from Edmonton
The fenced 200-km² park east of Edmonton provides a protected habitat for a large herd of Plains bison, moose, Wapiti deer and more than 200 bird species. *⊞ L11*

7 JURASSIC FOREST
40km / 30 mins by car north from Edmonton
This amazing adventure playground for dinosaur fans of all ages features true-to-life, moving models of many dino species in a primeval forest. *Daily 9am–7pm | admission C$15, children C$10 | 2-23210 Township Road 564 | Gibbons | jurassicforest.com | ⊞ L11*

8 REYNOLDS-ALBERTA MUSEUM
60km / 45 mins by car south from Edmonton
This museum traces the mechanisation of transport in Alberta, and exhibits historical farming equipment, airplanes, cars, etc. *Daily 10am–5pm, in winter closed Mon | admission*

The gigantic Edmonton Mall has 800 shops and attractions

C$13 | Wetaskiwin | reynoldsmuseum.ca | ◫ K–L12

Sands Discovery Centre (daily in summer 9am–5pm, otherwise Tue–Sun 10am–4pm | admission C$11).

FORT MCMURRAY

(◫ L9) **Out in the wilderness of northern Alberta, Fort McMurray (pop. 70,000) is an oil production hub. It is estimated that there are 27 billion tons of oil in the tar sands below the city, which are exploited using sometimes controversial methods and also by open-pit mining**.

In the 1960s an oil plant was established here in the midst of the endless forest, and from then on a city emerged. Those interested in technology can visit the state-of-the-art *Oil*

FANTASTICAL DREAMS
This kitsch bonanza is worth seeing: 120 of the 355 rooms of the *Fantasyland Hotel (17700 87th Av. | tel. 780 4 44 30 00 | flh.ca | C$$$)* are designed according to different themes. Whether you've always dreamt of sleeping Hollywood-style, or perhaps in an Arabian dream, or with South Pacific romance, or maybe in a spaceship or even in the back of a truck, then you've come to the right place!

NORTHERN TERRITORIES

VAST, BARREN & BEAUTIFUL

For wilderness enthusiasts and nature lovers, the region north of the 60th latitude is the most spectacular part of Canada. It is a raw, largely untouched land whose austere beauty provides ample material for tales of trappers, prospectors and lost expeditions.

Above all, it is a truly vast country (*spectacularNWT.com*). There are few highways and on these you will often not meet another soul for hours. However, the west of the region has been developed with

Dog sled on frozen Laberge Lake

several roads to the mountainous Yukon Territory. The greatest gold rush of all time took place one hundred years ago along the Klondike River in this territory. You can also reach the Northwest Territories that stretch along the huge and remote Mackenzie River valley and the Great Slave Lake. Only about 36,000 people live in the Yukon and 80,000 in the Northwest Territories. Despite good tourist facilities in the territories' small towns, adequate equipment and careful planning are essential for a trip to Northern Canada.

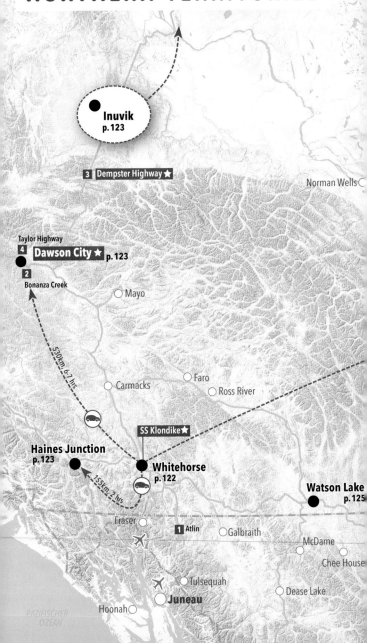

NORTHERN TERRITORIES

Inuvik
p. 123

3 Dempster Highway ★

Norman Wells

Taylor Highway
4 Dawson City ★ p. 123
2
Bonanza Creek

Mayo

530 km, 6.7 hrs

Carmacks

Faro

Ross River

SS Klondike ★

Haines Junction
p. 123

155 km, 2 hrs

Whitehorse
p. 122

Watson Lake
p. 125

Fraser

1 Atlin

Galbraith

McDame

Chee House

Tulsequah

Dease Lake

Juneau

Hoonah

PAZIFISCHER
OZEAN

MARCO POLO HIGHLIGHTS

★ **SS KLONDIKE**
An original paddle steamer from the good old gold rush days of yore ➤ p. 122

★ **DAWSON CITY**
The gold rush city in the Klondike is still a bustling small town ➤ p. 123

★ **DEMPSTER HIGHWAY**
The famed, 700-km wilderness road runs north from Dawson City all the way to the Polar Sea ➤ p. 124

★ **PRINCE OF WALES NORTHERN HERITAGE CENTRE**
A must-see museum: learn about the Northern Lights and indigenous cultures ➤ p. 127

Déline

CANADA

Gameti

1880km, 29 hrs

Whatì

Behchokǫ̀

Yellowknife ● p. 127
Prince of Wales Northern Heritage Centre ★

Mackenzie River

Great Slave Lake

6 Nahanni Nat. park

Hay River

Toad River Post

5 Muncho Lake   Snake River

Zama City

Wood Buffalo Nat. Park **7**

Rainbow Lake

Fox Lake

Fontas

UNITED STATES

✈

100 km
62.14 mi

WHITEHORSE

(□ C4) **Yukon's busy capital (pop. 25,000) stretches out along the broad banks of the Yukon River.**

Its first period of prosperity was around 1900. At that time, thousands of prospectors arrived on crude rafts and boats through the hazardous *Miles Canyon* and on their way to the gold fields of the Klondike. You can learn more about Whitehorse's golden era in the *MacBride Museum*

SIGHTSEEING

SS KLONDIKE ★
Built in 1937, this magnificent paddle steamer has been lovingly restored and now resides in a dry dock on the banks of the Yukon River. *Daily in summer 9.30am–5pm | admission free | guided tour C$6 | 2nd Av. | ◷ 1 hr*

YUKON WILDLIFE PRESERVE 🐾
This is the perfect opportunity to see the wild animals of the North up close: moose, bison, caribou and a dozen other species live in large enclosures. *Daily in summer 9.30am–6pm | admission C$22, children C$10 | Takhini Hot Springs Rd | yukonwildlife. ca | □ C4*

EATING & DRINKING

THE DECK
A popular bar with a terrace in the Coast Inn. There's a BBQ grill and wonderfully cold beer: choose from the clear Yukon Gold or the hoppy opaque Grizzly wheat beer. *4051 4th Av. | tel. 867 6 67 44 71 | C$$*

KLONDIKE RIB & SALMON BBQ
Rustic restaurant in an old pioneer cabin; good chowder, salmon and bison steaks. *2116 2nd Av. | tel. 867 6 67 75 54 | C$$$*

SPORT & ACTIVITIES

KANOE PEOPLE
Here you will get all the equipment you need for a leisurely canoe trip on the Yukon to Dawson City, including canoes, tents, etc. Guided tours available. *1147 1st Av. | tel. 867 6 68 48 99 | kanoepeople.com*

YUKON WILD
For rafting, canoeing and dog sledding, visit the joint website of approx. 20 adventure companies in the Yukon: *yukonwild.com*.

AROUND WHITEHORSE

① ATLIN
170km / 3 hrs by car from Whitehorse
The magnificent location, surrounded by mountains on the shores of Atlin Lake, makes the trip south to Atlin well worthwhile. The picturesque gold-mining village (founded in 1898 during the Klondike gold rush) is actually located in British Columbia, but it can be accessed only from the Yukon Territory. Today, around 500 people

Fur collars recommended: winter lasts for seven months in the Yukon

live in and around Atlin: gold prospectors, artists and people wanting to live an alternative lifestyle. ⚏ *C5*

HAINES JUNCTION

(⚏ *B4)* **The tiny village, surrounded by mountains, where the Alaska Highway meets the Haines Highway is a good starting point for trips to the Kluane National Park. The park covers 22,000km² of pristine mountain wilderness in the west of the Yukon.**

Canada's highest peak, *Mount Logan* (5,959m), is in the ice-covered St Elias Mountains on the border with Alaska. The Alaska Highway runs along the northern edge of the park (*visitor centre* in Haines Junction) on the banks of the 400 km² *Kluane Lake*. In the east of the park, the region around Kathleen Lake is beautiful for

hiking. Excursions by plane over icy ranges and overnight stays in a glacier camp up in the *St Elias Mountains* can be booked at *Icefield Discovery (from C$250 | tel. 867 8 41 42 04 | icefielddiscovery.com).*

DAWSON CITY

(⚏ *B1)* ★ **The gold rush era lives on in this practically deserted town that was known in the 1900s as the "Paris of the North".**

About 30,000 people lived here during the *Klondike Gold Rush*, but today this town at the mouth of the Klondike River in the Yukon is a Historic Site characterised by Wild West sidewalks and wooden façades. There are now only around 2,000 inhabitants in Dawson City; their income comes mainly from tourism, but the current high price of gold has once again drawn *miners* to the surrounding goldfields. For the best views follow the gravel road up to the *Midnight Dome*, a 1,000-m-high lookout point.

SIGHTSEEING

DAWSON CITY MUSEUM

The museum depicts the gold rush era with old photos, mining equipment and tools, film showings and gold panning demos. *Daily in summer 10am–6pm | admission C$9 | 5th Av./ Church St | ⊙ 2 hrs*

HISTORIC DISTRICT 🐖

Cancan girls dance in *Diamond Tooth Gertie's Gambling Hall*, while dramas are performed at the *Palace Grand Theatre*, and, in *Jack London's Cabin*, photos, documents and letters bring his novels to life. Many of the renovated old buildings are open to the public, such as the old *post office (King Street)*, the elegant *Commissioner's Residence (guided tours | Front Street)* and the historic *paddle steamer SS Keno* on the Yukon River. Every day at 1.15pm you can listen to a recital of amusing poetry by Robert Service, the bard of Klondike.

INSIDER TIP
Dawson City in prose

EATING & DRINKING

KLONDIKE KATE'S

This cosy pub in a historic building with a terrace serves great steaks and Sunday brunch. Cabins for hire. *3rd Av./King St | tel. 867 9 93 65 27 | C$$*

AROUND DAWSON CITY

2 BONANZA CREEK

5km / 20 mins by car from Dawson City

In 1896, the first gold was discovered south of Dawson City in the Klondike River valley. At Bonanza Creek an enormous tailings pile and the vast gold-panning plant – *Dredge No. 4* – bear witness to the hard lives of the gold diggers. ▥ B1

3 DEMPSTER HIGHWAY ★ ▐

More than 700km / 2 days by car from Dawson City

This gravel road runs from Dawson City to the deserted tundra regions north of the Arctic Circle, to the Inuit settlement of *Inuvik* in the Mackenzie Delta and, since 2017, on to the Arctic Ocean at Tuktoyaktuk. There are only two tiny First Nation villages and a petrol station along the entire route. The highway is especially scenic at the time of the midnight sun in June and in early September, when autumn transforms the tundra into a sea of colour. ▥ B–C1

4 TOP OF THE WORLD HIGHWAY/TAYLOR HIGHWAY

270km / 5 hrs by car from Dawson City

This, the most scenic connection between the Yukon and Alaska, is a panoramic ride through isolated mountain peaks, verdant valleys and old gold-mining areas. There is only one place to stop along the way: the old mining hamlet of *Chicken* in Alaska. At *Tok*, Highway 9 connects to the Alaska Highway, making a round trip back to Whitehorse possible *(road only open from late May–Sept).* ⊞ *A–B1*

INUVIK

(⊞ *0*) **About 3,000 people (Inuit, Dene and other cultures) live here on the eastern edge of the vast Mackenzie Delta, and the town lives up to its name of "Place of the People".**

However, beyond Inuvik, it pays to continue driving for another 180km to the Inuit settlement of *Tuktoyaktuk* on the Arctic Ocean. Take Canada's only road to the polar sea: at the very end of the road, which was only opened in 2017, is a monument with views out to sea.

INSIDER TIP
Polar sea panorama

WATSON LAKE

(⊞ *E5*) **Since the construction of the Alaska Highway in 1942, the village of Watson Lake (pop. 800) in the southern Yukon has become an important supply base.**

It is also home to the *Watson Lake Signpost Forest*, with 80,000 signposts from all over the world, started 75 years ago by a homesick soldier. Next to it is a modern *Interpretive Centre* that details the history of the Alaska Highway.

Today, it's not so much gold diggers as tourists that come to Dawson City

AROUND WATSON LAKE

5 MUNCHO LAKE

300km / 4 hrs by car from Watson Lake

This 11km-long, emerald-green lake lies south-east on the Alaska Highway (in British Columbia). Stop off at the *Liard Hot Springs* and soak away the dust of the wilderness. 🖽 *F6*

6 NAHANNI NAT. PARK

300km / 1 hr by airplane from Watson Lake

The park is an hour's flight northeast of Watson Lake and is a popular white-water rafting destination: the *South Nahanni River* runs through the *Mackenzie Mountains* before thundering over the 90-m-high *Virginia Falls* and into 900-m-deep gorges. In Whitehorse, companies such as *Nahanni River Adventures (tel. 867 6 68 31 80 | nahanni.com)* offer guided canoe trips and wilderness expeditions. Starting at the *Northern Rockies Lodge (mile 462 | tel. 250 7 76 34 81 | northernrockieslodge)* on the Alaska Highway, the Swiss bush pilot Urs Schildknecht offers impressive flying safaris to the park's waterfalls. 🖽 *F–G4–5*

INSIDER TIP
Fly into the wilderness

The bison herd in the Wood Buffalo National Park is 6,000 strong

YELLOWKNIFE

(🗺 K4) **You have the best views over the modern capital of the Northwest Territories from** *Pilot's Monument,* **on the brow of a hill.**

There are about 19,000 inhabitants and they are either state employees or involved in the two gold mines. Around 1990, diamonds were also discovered here and these are now prospected in large open-cast mines.

SIGHTSEEING

PRINCE OF WALES NORTHERN HERITAGE CENTRE ★
Arguably the best museum in the Northwest Territories, the centre has exhibits about the flora and fauna of the Arctic, and Yellowknife, which is a great place to see the Northern Lights. *Daily in summer 10.30am–5pm | admission free | Frame Lake St/48th St |* ⏱ *1.5 hrs*

EATING & DRINKING

DANCING MOOSE CAFE
Eggs Benedict for breakfast, delicious paninis and wraps for lunch. This popular restaurant in a wooden cabin by the lake is open all day, but not for dinner. With B&B. *3505 McDonald Dr. | tel. 867 4 45 50 03 | baysidenorth.com | C$*

THE WILDCAT CAFÉ
An institution: hearty pioneer cuisine and caribou steaks. *3904 Wylie Rd | tel. 867 8 73 40 04 | C$$*

AROUND YELLOWKNIFE

🔟 WOOD BUFFALO NAT. PARK
700km / 1 day by car from Yellowknife
The 45,000-km² reserve in the delta of the Peace and Athabasca rivers is the largest national park in Canada. The endless forests are home to 6,000 wild bison while the numerous water birds inhabit the wetlands, including rare cranes and the longest bird native to North America, the American white pelican.

Some gravel tracks lead from *Fort Smith (visitor centre)* into the reserve. You can also take a cruise on the Slave River. 🗺 *L8*

WHERE TO STAY IN THE NORTHERN TERRITORIES

A FORMER BROTHEL
Staying in a former brothel has its own charm, although the pub at *Bombay Peggy's (9 rooms | Princess St/2nd Av. | tel. 867 9 93 69 69 | bombaypeggys.com | C$$)* can be noisy at times.

DREAM LODGE
The *Inn on the Lake (8 rooms | Alaska Hwy Km 1,415 | tel. 867 6 60 52 53 | innonthelake.ca | C$$–$$$)* near Whitehorse is perfect: idyllic location, lovely log-cabin architecture and excellent cuisine.

DISCOVERY TOURS

Want to get under the skin of the region? Then our discovery tours provide the perfect guide – they provide advice on which sights to visit, tips on where to stop for that perfcet holiday snap, a choice of the best places to eat and drink and suggestions for fun activities.

❶ FROM THE PRAIRIES TO THE PACIFIC

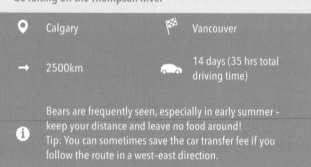

- ➤ Drive through the Rockies on the glacier route
- ➤ Taste Canadian wine in the Okanagan Valley
- ➤ Go rafting on the Thompson River

📍	Calgary	🏁	Vancouver
→	2500km	🚗	14 days (35 hrs total driving time)

ℹ️ Bears are frequently seen, especially in early summer – keep your distance and leave no food around!
Tip: You can sometimes save the car transfer fee if you follow the route in a west–east direction.

Rain forest in British Columbia

SHOPPING, DINOSAUR DISCOVERIES & SNOW-COVERED PEAKS

A day to get settled in ❶ Calgary ➤ p. 106: stroll in Stephen Avenue Mall, visit the Heritage Park and shop cheaply as there is no provincial tax in Alberta. The next morning, make the most of the great clothes and shoes bargains at 🐷 Crossiron Mills a huge discount mall *at the north end of the city (Hwy 2, Exit 273).* Now it's time to *head east on Hwys 567 and 9 into the wide plains and to* ❷ Drumheller ➤ p. 111 and the spectacular dinosaur finds in the Valley of the Red Deer River. Do you fancy making some prehistoric discoveries of your own? The 👥 experienced guides of the great Royal Tyrrell Museum ➤ p. 111 offer half-day excursions that are exciting not just for small children.

The next day, *on your way back, take Hwys 56 and 1.* The exhibition at the ❸ Blackfoot Crossing Historical Park ➤ p. 110 is well worth a stop, as is a bison burger in the café of the First Nations Museum. *Head west via Calgary:* the ❹ Trans-Canada Highway *runs along Bow River from the plains to the Rocky Mountains,* crossing the old tribal land of the Blackfoot First Nations. Soon you'll see the rugged snowy peaks of the Rockies

| DAY 1 |
| ❶ Calgary |

| DAYS 2-3 |
| 140km 1.5 hrs |
| ❷ Drumheller |
| 100km 1 hr |

| ❸ Blackfoot Crossing Historical Park |
| 130km 90 mins |

| ❹ Trans-Canada Highway |
| 105km 1 hr |

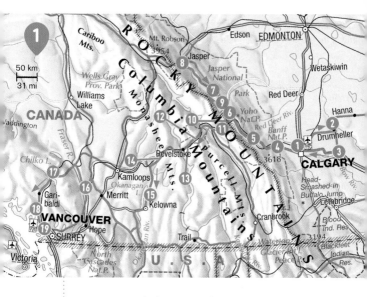

on the horizon. *By the time you're near Canmore, the mountains are closer to Hwy 1 and appear ever higher.*

BANFF & JASPER NATIONAL PARK: A HIKER'S DREAM

DAYS 4–5
⑤ Banff National Park
240km   3 hrs

Directly behind the first sign that warns of bears is the entrance to ⑤ Banff National Park ➤ p. 88, – the oldest and most famous conservation area in the Rocky Mountains. You should plan to stay for two nights in Banff , so you have time for some hiking in the mountains – at the Vermilion Lakes right on the outskirts of Banff or near Lake Louise, Moraine Lake and Johnston Canyon. The panoramic bar and terrace of the historic Banff Springs Hotel, overlooking the valley of the Bow River, are perfect for an evening drink.

DAYS 6–7
⑥ Icefields Parkway
65km   1 hr

The next leg of your route covers the most beautiful panoramic road in the Rocky Mountains: the ⑥ Icefields Parkway ➤ p. 88. It is a splendidly constructed route that runs parallel to the mountain ridges to the north. Keep your camera at the ready, as you will get some spectacular shots: the narrow gorge of the Mistaya River and the panoramic views at Waterfowl Lake are especially beautiful.

Follow the steep climb to the 2,035-m Sunwapta Pass and, if the weather is good, take a two-hour walk on the ❼ Parker Ridge Trail before *the route leads by the* Athabasca Glacier ➤ p. 94 *to the* ❽ Jasper National Park ➤ p. 94. You should stop here for another day: hike in the Maligne Canyon ➤ p. 95, take a cable car ride to the summit above the city and a boat cruise on Maligne Lake.

❼ Parker Ridge Trail	
115 km	1.5 hrs
❽ Jasper National Park	
325km	4 hrs

CROSSING THE ROCKY MOUNTAINS' RIDGE

Back to the south: you will be amazed how different the mountains look when you are on your way back. You should get up early for the *return trip on Icefields Parkway*. If you are lucky and the weather is good, the sun will light up the peaks in an early alpenglow, and quite often you can observe bears and mountain sheep along the road. At lunchtime, stop off at the historic trapper lodge ❾ Num-Ti-Jah ➤ p. 90 on Bow Lake. *From Lake Louise, follow Hwy 1 westwards across the ridge of the Rockies to British Columbia (1-hour time difference) and into the* ❿ Yoho National Park ➤ p. 97, where the highest waterfalls in the Rocky Mountains, the Takakkaw Falls ➤ p. 98, shoot from the Waputik Icefield in an impressive arch. Treat yourself to a canoe trip or a walk around the idyllic ⓫ Emerald Lake before stopping at Field for the night,

DAY 8	
❾ Num-Ti-Jah	
65km	1 hr
❿ Yoho National Park	
30km	45 mins
⓫ Emerald Lake	

Icefields Parkway is without doubt one of the most scenic roads in Canada

for example at the Truffle Pigs ➤ p. 98 with its excellent restaurant. You will find more good motels and B&Bs in Golden.

DAYS 9-10
175km 2 hrs

WESTWARDS ON THE TRANS-CANADA HIGHWAY

Travel via Golden (time zone: –1 hour), through the jagged mountain range of the Columbia Mountains in the ⑫ Glacier National Park ➤ p. 79. *This is immediately followed by the smaller* ⑬ Revelstoke National Park ➤ p. 77. If you take this route in midsummer, you should head to the flower meadows and the magnificent hiking trails near the summits. After you've stayed a night in Revelstoke, you must pass the densely forested Monashee Mountains. Deep in the forests is a place called Craigellachie, a historic train station where the final nail of the Trans-Canada Railway line was hammered in on 9 November 1885.

⑫ Glacier
National Park
45km 40 mins

⑬ Revelstoke
National Park
95km 1.5 hrs

TIME FOR A TREAT

Shortly afterwards, in ⑭ Sicamous, it would be a sin to miss the 🍦Dutchman Dairy *(1321 Maier Rd)* – those giant scoops of ice cream do taste phenomenally good. In Sicamous, *the route branches off south from Hwy 1, into the* ⑮ Okanagan Valley ➤ p. 72. All those wineries along Hwy 97 around the towns of Kelowna and Penticton make exceedingly fine wine. It's pleasure time now: tastings in *wineries*, followed by delicious lunches in terrace bars and bathing in warm lakes. Tip: *take the Boucherie Road west of Kelowna on the western shore of the Okanagan Lake* to wineries such as Quails' Gate and Mission Hill ➤ p. 73. To end the day, take your time to enjoy an evening stroll along the bustling beach promenade in Penticton.

⑭ Sicamous
100km 1.5 hrs

⑮ Okanagan Valley
400km 5 hrs

NOW COMES THE SPORTY PART:
RAFTING, CYCLING OR GOLF

The ranch land of British Columbia comes after Penticton: it is dry like a desert and almost always sunny. *The route will now wind northwards along Hwys 5A, 8 and 1* through rolling hills and large cattle pastures to the Fraser River Canyon. If it's a hot summer's day you should go rafting at ⑯ Lytton ➤ p. 76. Hyak

DAYS 11-14

⑯ Lytton

Rafting *(C$140| tel. 600 7 34 86 22 | hyak.com)* offer an afternoon tour that should be perfect for your timing. *Hwy 99 climbs from the river across the sparsely populated Coast Mountains westwards and leads to* ⑰ Whistler ➤ p. 68, the alpine venue of the 2010 Olympic Winter Games. It's time for a ride to Whistler Mountain, a bike or zip-line tour or a round of golf. Continue the next morning and at Squamish you'll see the sea at Howe Sound. You get an even better view from the ⑱ Sea to Sky Gondola *(36800 Hwy 99)* which takes you 885m above the fjord in ten minutes. Trails, a spectacular rope bridge and a restaurant await you at the top. *From here it's only an hour's drive of beautiful panoramas on Hwy 99 to* ⑲ Vancouver ➤ p. 38, where you should plan another day for sightseeing.

190km	2.5 hrs
⑰ Whistler	
62km	1 hr
⑱ Sea to Sky Gondola	
60km	1 hr
⑲ Vancouver	

❷ VANCOUVER ISLAND: BEACHES & RAINFOREST

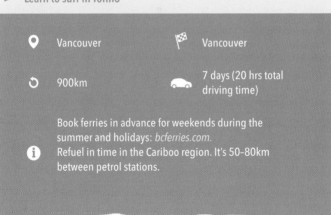

➤ See some of Western Canada's most beautiful sights
➤ Watch orcas on a fast boat trip
➤ Learn to surf in Tofino

📍 Vancouver   🏁 Vancouver

↻ 900km   🚗 7 days (20 hrs total driving time)

ℹ Book ferries in advance for weekends during the summer and holidays: *bcferries.com.*
Refuel in time in the Cariboo region. It's 50–80km between petrol stations.

DAY 1

❶ Vancouver

115km 3 hrs

DAYS 2-3

❷ Victoria

80km 90 mins

URBAN FLAIR & COLOURFUL GARDENS

Start in ❶ Vancouver ➤ p. 38. You should plan at least one day for the most beautiful metropolis in West Canada: do some sightseeing in Gastown, on Granville Island and in Robson Street, take a bike tour in Stanley Park, and, of course, go out for a fine dinner of fresh wild salmon. In South Vancouver, the *large car ferries that are operated by BC Ferries run almost every hour from the ferry terminal in Tsawwassen to* Vancouver Island ➤ p. 50. Keep your eyes open, as orcas are sometimes seen on this mini cruise through the archipelago of the Gulf Islands. At the *port of Swartz Bay, head south on Hwy 17 to* ❷ Victoria ➤ p. 54, the gorgeous provincial capital of British Columbia, or BC as it is locally called. The casual and fun atmosphere of this seaside town will become evident on your first stroll in the afternoon around the Inner Harbour and the beautiful old town – the motto seems to be "easy living". The totem poles of the Royal BC Museum are not to be missed. The next morning, take a boat trip and do some whale watching, as the islands just off the coast are home to several pods of orcas throughout the summer. How about a bike ride through the lush

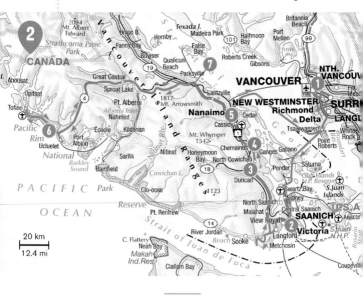

Street art: one of the magnificent murals in Chemainus

residential area of Victoria in the afternoon? Bike rental is available at the shop Sports Rent *(1950 Government St)*. If you like hiking, then take a trip to East Sooke Park, which is just an hour's drive west of downtown *(you get there via Hwy 14 and East Sooke Rd)*. Here, a beautiful trail starts from the Pike Road parking lot and leads to wonderfully secluded bays.

INSIDER TIP
Sea view in a remote location

FISH & CHIPS AT TROLLERS, A BOAT TOUR & MARVELLOUS BEACHES

Continue your trip on the *Trans-Canada Highway*. On the outskirts of Victoria is the Goldstream Park where, in the autumn, salmon swim to their spawning grounds and then die in the shallows: it's an impressive spectacle. *Continue north: pass the 350-m-high Malahat summit* that offers panoramic views across the sea, and then *head for* ❸ Duncan ➤ p. 56 where you can admire the many totem poles. *Continue on the route to* ❹ Chemainus, famous for its *murals* that were created by internationally renowned artists. At ❺ Nanaimo ➤

DAY 4

❸ Duncan
18km   20 mins
❹ Chemainus
35km   30 mins
❺ Nanaimo

p. 58 stop for a nice stroll by the harbour and some fish and chips at Trollers *(104 Front St | C$)*, a popular hangout at the harbour pier. *Follow Hwys 19 and 4 for just under three hours to the west coast of Vancouver Island* and the ❻ Pacific Rim National Park ➤ p. 58 with its steep cliffs and untouched rainforest. On the way you can stop to relax and enjoy the ancient Douglas fir trees at Cathedral Grove. When you reach the coast, it is a good idea to find somewhere to stay in the former fishing village of Tofino, on the edge of the national park. The accommodation with the most beautiful view is certainly the cosy Middle Beach Lodge *(64 rooms | 400 MacKenzie Beach Rd. | tel. 250 7 25 29 00 | middle beach.com | C$$)*. In two days you can go for a walk along Long Beach, take a boat tour for bear watching, a hike on the Wild Pacific Trail in Ucluelet – and maybe a half-day surf course. *Take Hwys 4 and 19 back to the east coast of the island.* Go for another dip off sandy ❼ Rathtrevor Provincial Park. In the afternoon, *take the ferry from Nanaimo back to* ❶ Vancouver.

Mastering a wave tunnel is every surfer's dream – here off Vancouver Island

❸ THE WEST COAST: FJORDS & GREEN ISLANDS

➤ Enter the realm of the First Nations, lumberjacks and pioneer farmers
➤ Sail the legendary Inside Passage
➤ Kayak in the Clayoquot Sound near Tofino

📍 Vancouver   🏁 Vancouver

🔄 4000km, of which 500km are by ferry   🚗 11 days (70 hrs total journey time)

ℹ️ In summer, you definitely need to book the ferry ride through the Inside Passage from ❻ Port Hardy to ❽ Prince Rupert in advance at *bcferries.com*

THE INSIDE PASSAGE – PREFERABLY IN SUNSHINE

Car ferries leave from the Horseshoe Bay terminal on the northern edge of ❶ Vancouver ➤ p. 38 *to* Vancouver Island ➤ p. 50. ❷ Nanaimo ➤ p. 58, *the destination port, has a very pretty harbour promenade.* Take Hwys 19 and 4 and head for the beautiful ❸ Pacific Rim National Park ➤ p. 58. The small town of Tofino *at the end of Hwy 4 is the best location to stay for two nights: for beach walks and maybe a boat ride or kayak trip.*

On the east coast, the route follows Hwy 19 via Campbell River ➤ p. 61 *to the north of Vancouver Island. Do not miss a whale watching tour from* ❹ Telegraph Cove ➤ p. 63 *and a ferry trip to* ❺ Alert Bay ➤ p. 62 *with its First Nation reservation museum, which has a magnificent collection of totem poles and indigenous masks. After a night in* ❻ Port Hardy ➤ p. 62, *embark on the trip through the* ❼ Inside Passage ➤ p. 62 – *with a bit of luck the sun will be*

DAYS 1–4		
❶ Vancouver		
	80km	2.5 hrs
❷ Nanaimo		
	170km	3 hrs
❸ Pacific Rim National Park		
	450km	6 hrs
❹ Telegraph Cove		
	55km	1.5 hrs
❺ Alert Bay		
	50km	1.5 hrs
DAYS 5–6		
❻ Port Hardy		
❼ Inside Passage		

520km 15 hrs

shining. It often rains along the sparsely populated coastline as the steep Coast Mountains capture the Pacific clouds. That is exactly why the towering Douglas fir and Sitka spruce thrive in the island labyrinth and on the mainland of the fjords, creating a unique forest. You can often watch whales, seals and bald eagles from the ferry.

GRIZZLIES IN THE FJORDS NEAR PRINCE RUPERT

You will reach **⑧** *Prince Rupert* ➤ *p. 81 after 15 hours.* The ferry port is in the land of the Tsimshan First Nation. Large totem poles throughout the city testify to their

⑧ Prince Rupert
450km 6 hrs

carving skills. Stay a day in Prince Rupert: in the morning take a bear-watching tour in the Khutzemateen Reserve with Prince Rupert Adventure Tours; in the afternoon head to the North Pacific Cannery *(July/Aug daily 10am–5pm, spring and autumn closed on Mon | admission C$12)* in the suburb of Port Edward, which impressively documents the long tradition of fishing in the region.

Continue on Hwy 16, the Yellowhead Highway ➤ p. 80. It runs along the often-cloudy Skeena River. *Plan a trip to Alaska from Terrace: a half-day trip on the Nisga'a and Cassiar highways leads to the town of* ❾ Stewart ➤ p. 82, that is located right on the border with Alaska. The little village of Hyder has rustic pubs and is visited in summer by bears that come to catch salmon at Fish Creek, on the outskirts of the village. In Stewart, the historic Ripley Creek Inn ➤ p. 82 is a good place to stay. *Head back to the Cassiar Highway and then south to* ❿ Hazelton, which is an important settlement of the Tsimshian First Nation who operate the very interesting K'san Outdoor Museum. Stop for the night shortly

DAYS 7–9

❾ Stewart

280km 4 hrs

❿ Hazelton

450km 5.5 hrs

Bears lie in wait for leaping salmon at Fish Creek

after this museum in Smithers. *The ride on the Yellowhead Highway is really long and seems to go on forever*, past lonely forests and lakes, and every now and then a small village. The next day, dead conifers on the roadside are evidence of the frantic spread of the bark beetle. South of the lumberjack town of ⑪ Prince George ➤ p. 81, the seemingly endless forests have suffered even more – huge forest fires raged here as recently as 2017. (You can connect to Route 1 on Hwy 16 and continue to the Rockies.)

LIKE AN OLD WESTERN

Head south on Hwy 97, the Cariboo Highway, through the sunny ranch land of the Cariboo Region ➤ p. 70. The old gold mining town of ⑫ Barkerville ➤ p. 70, is not to be missed. It is completely preserved as a Ghost Town Museum and a site of historic interest. *From the 100 Mile House, take Hwys 24 and 5 to Clearwater and the* ⑬ Wells Gray Provincial Park ➤ p. 79 which is famous for its waterfalls and lakes. Make sure you have time for a canoe trip on Clearwater Lake. *On the way back, take Hwy 5 back to civilisation and to the mostly sunny and hot ranch land around* Kamloops ➤ p. 75. In the valley of the Thompson River, *the Trans-Canada Highway meanders westwards.*

The dry *interior* of BC is almost desert-like and looks like a location from a Western movie. Visit ⑭ Hat Creek Ranch *(May–Sept daily 9am–5pm | admission C$13.50)* near Cache Creek; it's an authentic and photogenic coaching inn. *Continue from* ⑮ Lytton ➤ p. 76 (where you still have time for a rafting trip) *on the Trans-Canada Highway, which follows the Fraser River to the sea.* The mighty river has carved a deep canyon through the Coast Mountains. The narrowest and wildest section of the river runs from south of Lytton to just before Hope. Near Hope, a short hike on an old railway track leads through the Othello Tunnels in the Coquihalla Canyon Park to a dramatic gorge. Dense forests cover the hillsides and accompany *Hwy 1 through the widening Fraser Valley back to* ① Vancouver.

INSIDER TIP
Tunnel view of the canyon

Timeline (sidebar)

⑪ **Prince George**
190km · 2.5 hrs

DAYS 10–11

⑫ **Barkerville**
430km · 5 hrs

⑬ **Wells Gray Provincial Park**
285km · 3.5 hrs

⑭ **Hat Creek Ranch**
95km · 90 mins

⑮ **Lytton**
260km · 3 hrs

① **Vancouver**

❹ YUKON'S GOLDEN ROUTE

➤ Follow the original route of the prospectors to the Klondike
➤ Hike to the legendary Chilkoot Pass and take a canoe to Dawson City
➤ Sit by a campfire in the wilderness

📍 Skagway, Alaska   🏁 Dawson City, Yukon

→ 53km by foot,
120km by bus/train,
736km by canoe   🚶 21 days

ℹ️ Best time to travel: July/Aug. The trail requires a permit from the *park service*. Registration and information at *nps.gov/klgo*. Booking recommended. In summer, a rail-bus service runs for hikers from ❹ Bennett to ❺ Whitehorse: *wpyr.com*.

THE ORIGINAL ROUTE OF THE PROSPECTORS

INSIDER TIP
Pure adventure

It sounds like a lot, but the 736-km canoe tour is suitable even for beginners because you comfortably drift along with the current. The 53-km hike at the beginning is much more strenuous. Alternatively, you can do it – or indeed the entire tour – by car.

DAYS 1-5

HIKE TO THE FAMOUS CHILKOOT PASS

The journey starts, as it once did for the pioneers, in Alaska in ❶ Skagway. *You can easily reach it by ferry or plane from the south and by bus from Whitehorse.* As in the old days, the little town is the last feeding station on the way into the hinterland. In the winter of 1898, 30,000 adventurers journeyed from Skagway across the mountains to the north and in the following spring to the Yukon River and on to the Klondike gold fields. *The route of the historic ❷ Chilkoot Trail, as well as the parallel modern highway, runs mostly through pristine wilderness.* Today, a *hike across the 1,067-m-high*

❶ Skagway

❷ Chilkoot Trail
38 km   2–3 days

❸ Chilkoot Pass takes four to five days and you can book a tent in advance. The prospectors, on the other hand, had to haul a ton of luggage across the pass as well as enough food and equipment for a full year. Mounties of the Canadian police checked at the summit of the pass whether each pioneer had brought the required quantity. In the dead of winter the pioneers had to climb the steep ridge of the Coast Mountains 30 or 40 times to laboriously haul up their luggage. This may serve as an incentive for today's hikers who work up a gentle summer sweat under a super-light high-tech backpack when crossing the pass... just the once, that is. The end point of the Chilkoot Trail is ❹ Bennett. *Continue by train and bus via Carcross to* ❺ Whitehorse ➤ p. 122.

The historic Chilkoot Trail starts at sea level and leads up above the tree line

A CANOE ON THE YUKON RIVER

Take a day of rest in the town of Whitehorse. In the paddle steamer SS Klondike ➤ p. 122 in Miles Canyon you can learn more about the historical sites of the gold rush era and stock up on your supplies. *Then head further north.* Now it becomes very authentic as you travel by canoe, just as the prospectors of the past would have used rafts and self-made boats to drift northwards down the Yukon River to the promised land of gold. Today, this route can be made by canoe in about 15 days and doesn't require much wilderness experience. Canoe rentals and suppliers can be found in Whitehorse and guided tours are organised by Ruby Range (rubyrange.com). *You slowly drift down the wide Yukon, paddling through* ❻ Lake Labarge, *observing moose and bear, trying (mostly unsuccessful) to catch some fish, mastering the* Five-Finger Rapids, *making campfires on the shore and enjoying the tranquillity of nature. Finally, you re-join civilisation at the town of* ❼ Dawson City ➤ p. 123, *where the Klondike River meets the Yukon: the destination at the end of the Golden Trail.*

DAYS 6–21	
50km	1–2 days
❻ Lake Labarge	
686km	14 days
❼ Dawson City	

GOOD TO KNOW

HOLIDAY BASICS

ARRIVAL

Time zones

Canada has several time zones. British Columbia and the Yukon are eight hours and Alberta is seven hours behind Greenwich Mean Time (GMT). The time-zone border basically runs along the ridge of the Rocky Mountains. Unlike Europe, summertime is from the second Sunday in March until the first Sunday in November.

Air Canada and most national carriers have regular direct flights to Vancouver or to Calgary with domestic flight connections to all the major cities. Other indirect locations, such as Edmonton and Whitehorse, can also be reached via connecting flights with other European airlines including Iceland Air.

It is possible to travel via Eastern Canada, although it is better to take direct flights to Western Canada (which last approx. 11 hours) because, once you add on a few additional hours for transfers, as well as the time difference the journey can become a bit too much.

In the peak tourist season (July and August) you should book the trans-Atlantic route as early as possible – several months in advance, if possible – as flights are often fully booked. (This also applies to motor homes and the ferry for the Inside Passage along the West Coast.)

GETTING IN

Tourists from the US, EU and most Commonwealth countries (UK, Australia and New Zealand) require a

Stanley Park in Vancouver

valid machine-readable passport and, since 2016, also an *Electronic Travel Authorization (ETA)*, which is valid for five years and available for C$7 at *canada.ca/eta*.

Check to see if you qualify under the *Visa Waiver Program (VWP)* if you plan to cross the border into the US (you can travel to the US for up to 90 days without having to obtain a visa).

Please note that children need their own passport even if registered in their parent's passport.

CLIMATE & WHEN TO GO

Apart from the coastal regions of British Columbia, Western Canada has an extreme continental climate with cold, snowy winters and dry, hot summers. The best time to travel (and high season) is mid-June to late August, but September is often just as nice. And in the autumn the vibrant colours of the leaves produce a stunning display. February and March are best for skiing in the Rockies.

GETTING AROUND

CAR HIRE

The major car rental companies like Alamo, Avis and Hertz have representatives at all airports. The minimum age to rent a car is sometimes 21 and frequently 25 years. Your national driving licence will suffice. You should book cars or camper vans through a travel agent several months in advance, this is usually cheaper and safer because taxes and insurance will be included in the price. Also, motorhomes are often fully booked in peak season. One-way routes frequently incur high return transfer fees.

When travelling with an RV or motorhome, it is advisable to spend the first night in a hotel in town. The hire company will pick you up the next morning – well-rested for your first trip with the potentially unfamiliar vehicle.

DRIVING

You can drive with your national driving license for up to three months (Yukon Territory: 1 month). In all provinces it is compulsory to wear seatbelts. On major roads the speed limits are 80kmh or 100kmh, in towns 50kmh and on motorways 110kmh.

Traffic regulations are standard but there are certain unusual features: at traffic lights you can turn right on red, on multi-lane roads you may overtake on the right, but school buses – when they have their hazard lights on – must never be passed, not even when approaching from the opposite direction. In the Yukon Territory you must have your lights on during the day.

If you break down or have an accident, you should contact the car rental company immediately, which will organise repairs or a courtesy car.

DOMESTIC FLIGHTS

It is advisable to book domestic flights with *Air Canada* together with your transatlantic ticket because you are often offered free 🐷 stopovers. Otherwise, flights on regional airlines such as *Air North* and *WestJet* are generally cheaper when purchased online.

FERRIES

Ferries travel hourly between Vancouver Island and the mainland and do not require advance booking. Expect waiting times at weekends and during the summer. However, you will need to book early for the 15-hour trip between Port Hardy and Prince Rupert through the Inside Passage (available from travel agencies and all Canada tour operators).

For further information once you are in Canada: *tel. 250 3 86 34 31 or 1 88 82 23 37 79 | bcferries.com*

PUBLIC TRANSPORT

There are no long-distance bus services such as *Greyhound* in Western Canada, but regional bus lines *(eg Brewster, Red Arrow Express, Pacific Coach Lines)* connect some of the larger towns.

Another wonderful way to see Canada is to travel by train from coast to coast on the legendary *Trans-Canada route* from Toronto via Jasper to Vancouver, and there is also the *Rocky Mountaineer* from Calgary via Banff to Vancouver (book several months in advance at *rocky mountaineer.com*). The rail company VIA Rail *(viarail.ca)* offers a 🐷 *Canrailpass* for their entire network.

EMERGENCIES

CONSULATES & EMBASSIES
BRITISH CONSULATE GENERAL
Suite 800, 1111 Melville St | Vancouver | BC V6E 3V6 | tel.

FESTIVALS & EVENTS
ALL YEAR ROUND

MAY

Cloverdale Rodeo (Vancouver): *cloverdalerodeo.com*
Victoria Day Parade (Victoria), *gvfs.ca*

JUNE

International Jazz Festival (Vancouver): *coastaljazz.ca*
Guy Weadick Days (High River): rodeo and pioneer wagon races, *highriverag.com*

JULY

Banff Arts Festival (Banff): classical concerts performed by young artists
Calgary Stampede (Calgary): world's biggest rodeo, *calgarystampede.com*
Marine Festival and Bathtub Race (Nanaimo): at the end of July, more than 100 wacky bathtubs paddle to Vancouver, *bathtubbing.com*
Vancouver Island Music Festival (Comox): *islandmusicfest.com*
Celebration of Light (Vancouver): spectacular fireworks over the bay (photo), *hondacelebrationoflight.com*

AUGUST

Squamish Days Logger Sports (Squamish): lumberjack competitions, *squamishdays.ca*
Whoop-up Days (Lethbridge): rodeo and Western folk festival, *exhibition park.ca/whoop-up-days*
Abbotsford International Airshow (Vancouver): modern jets and historical biplanes, *abbotsfordairshow.com*
Discovery Days (Dawson City): *dawsoncity.ca/events*
Edmonton Fringe Festival: alternative theatre performances, *fringe theatre.ca*
Pacific National Exhibition (Vancouver): fair, country music, *pne.ca*

SEPTEMBER

Langley Cruise-In (Langley): vintage car parade, *langleycruise-in.com*
Klondike International Outhouse Race (Dawson City): prospectors in original costumes parade decorated loos through the town, *dawsoncity.ca/events*

604 6 83 4421 | www.gov.uk/world/organisations/british-consulate-general-vancouver

US CONSULATE GENERAL
1095 W Pender St | Vancouver | BC V6E 2M6 | tel. 604 6 85 43 11 | ca.usembassy.gov/embassy-consulates/vancouver

AUSTRALIAN CONSULATE
Suite 2050-1075 | West Georgia St | Vancouver | BC V6E 3C9 | tel. +1 604 6 94 61 60 | www.canada.embassy. gov.au

EMERGENCY SERVICES
Call 911 for the *police*, *fire service* and *ambulance*, or 0 for the *operator*.

HEALTH
Medical care in Canada is excellent but expensive. Make sure that you have health insurance for travelling abroad. You can buy medicine in a *pharmacy* or *drugstore* as well as in larger supermarkets.

ESSENTIALS

ALCOHOL/CANNABIS
In British Columbia, the legal age for drinking alcohol is 19, and in Alberta it's 18. Some supermarkets sell beer and wine, but spirits are only available in special *liquor stores*. The same age limits and similar restrictions on sale apply to the private consumption of cannabis which has been permitted in Canada since 2018. However, any other drugs continue to be strictly prohibited in Canada.

CAMPING & YOUTH HOSTELS
Canada's public campsites are beautiful. They are usually situated next to the water in national parks and they all have a firepit, wooden benches, water pump and a simple outhouse and cost C$10–40 per night. Private, luxuriously equipped sites can be found on the outskirts of cities and outside the national parks (prices approx. C$20–70). Camping rough is not prohibited (except in the parks) but is frowned upon in populated areas. Camping spaces in national parks can be booked in advance at *reservation.pc.gc.ca*; other parks in British Columbia at *discovercamping. ca*. There aren't many youth hostels in Canada although there are several ☛ hostels in beautiful locations in the parks of the Rockies. The *Canadian Hostelling Association website (hihostels.ca) provides information.*

CUSTOMS
It is prohibited to take plants and fresh foodstuffs into Canada. Each person is allowed 200 cigarettes, 50 cigars and 200g tobacco as well as 1.14l of spirits, 1.5l wine, plus gifts up to a value of C$60 per recipient.

Duty-free when returning to the UK is 4 litres spirits (over 22 per cent), 200 cigarettes or 50 cigars or 250g tobacco and other goods worth up to £390.

INTERNET & WIFI

Canada has an excellent network. Hotels often provide free internet access, only luxury hotels charge a fee for ultra-fast connections. Computers in the lobby are often available free of charge. With your own laptop or smart phone you find WiFi (free or with a password from the staff) in many coffee shops. You are also able to surf free of charge and check your e-mails in most *visitor centres* and all *public libraries*.

MOBILE PHONES

Most tri- or quad-band European mobiles only function in cities and in the south of the Provinces (sometimes subject to high roaming charges), while networks can be surprisingly patchy in the vast hinterland. Ask your

INSIDER TIP
Get a holiday deal

mobile phone provider about special rates and add-on data options before travelling.

It's cheaper to use phone booths or *prepaid long distance phone cards* than using your mobile. Cards are available at *petrol stations* and in *grocery stores*. For a long stay it is worth getting a Canadian SIM card and using it with your (unlocked!) mobile.

MONEY & CREDIT CARDS

The local currency is the Canadian dollar (= 100 cents). Bank notes are available in 5, 10, 20, 50 and 100 dollars and coins in ¢1 *(penny)*, ¢5 *(nickel)*, ¢10 *(dime)*, ¢25 *(quarter)* as well as C$1 and C$2. For current exchanges rates and a currency calculator please visit xe.com.

HOW MUCH DOES IT COST?

Coffee	C$2.50–4
	for a cup of coffee
Beer	C$5.50–8.25
	for a glass in a bar
Salmon	C$16.50–34.25
	for a salmon dish in a restaurant
Boots	C$165–180
	for a pair of original cowboy boots
Petrol	C$1.25–1.30
	for 1 litre regular unleaded
Canoe	C$20–35
	for 1 hour's rental

You can exchange foreign currencies into dollars at airports and in major hotels (although the rate may be poor), but not in banks. Visa or Mastercard is accepted everywhere at petrol stations, in restaurants, etc.), as well as a debit cards which you can use to draw cash from most ATMs at a favourable exchange rate. Traveller's cheques are accepted in shops and restaurants and you get your change in cash.

MOSQUITOES

These whining little monsters can turn hikes and camping holidays into hell, particularly in early summer. Luckily, these insects do not transmit any diseases and even the bite of the *black flies* is unpleasant but not dangerous. The best protection is to use Canadian repellents containing DEET such as Off, Cutter or Muskol.

OPENING HOURS

Shops are usually open Monday–Saturday 9.30am–6pm, large shopping malls 10am–9pm and Sunday noon–5pm. Supermarkets are often open evenings and weekends, in the large cities some are open around the clock. Many museums are closed on Mondays.

POST

Most post offices are open Monday–Friday 9am–5.30pm and Saturday 8am–noon. Drugstores often have post offices as well. A card to Europe takes approx. five days from major cities and nine days from the hinterland.

PUBLIC HOLIDAYS

1 Jan	New Year's Day
March/April	Good Friday, Easter Monday
Mon before 25 May	Victoria Day
1 July	Canada Day (national day)
1st Mon in Aug	Provincial holiday in British Columbia and Alberta
3rd Mon in Aug	Discovery Day (Yukon Territory)
1st Mon in Sept	Labour Day
2nd Mon in Oct	Thanksgiving
11 Nov	Remembrance Day
25/26 Dec	Christmas

SMOKING

There is a smoking ban in all public buildings, at airports and in restaurants. Smoking is extremely expensive and is no longer regarded as acceptable.

TAX

Canada has a 5% *Goods and Services Tax (GST)* levied by the federal government (basically a value-added tax), and each province has its own *Provincial Sales Tax (PST)*. British Columbia has a PST of 7%. There is also a hotel tax. Some taxes are only added to the purchase price at the cash register.

TELEPHONE NUMBERS

All Canadian telephone numbers have seven digits, i.e. a three-digit *area code* plus a seven-digit number. For long-distance calls within Canada, dial an additional "1" before the area code. If you have problems phoning, talk to the *operator* (dial "0"). Toll-free numbers (eg for booking a hotel or tour) start with 800, 866, 877 or 888.

If you want to call a number in the UK, dial 01144, followed by the UK's area code, omitting the initial "0". Then dial the actual number.

For calling a number in Canada from the UK, dial 001 plus the Canadian number.

Telephone booths have almost disappeared, with a few exceptions at airports as well as in malls and hotels. Local calls are charged between C$1–2, whereas for long-distance calls the fee is announced after you have dialled.

TIPPING

A service charge is not included in restaurants, and the standard tip is 15–20% of the invoice amount. Hotel porters get about C$1–2 per item of luggage.

TOURIST INFORMATION

Canadian Tourist Office website *www.canada.travel* provides extensive information about Canada's attractions and activities. There are competitions, travel ideas and links to the individual provinces such as Alberta and British Columbia, and you can also request brochures and maps for each region.

More detailed information and suggestions for tours in individual provinces and territories are available on their websites.

Alberta: *travelalberta.com*
British Columbia: *britishcolumbia.travel* and *www.hellobc.com*
Yukon: *travelyukon.com*

Electricity – adapter types A & B

Current is 110 volts, 60Hz. Mobile phones, tablets and appliances such as shavers and hair dryers from other countries will need a transformer and you will also need a plug adaptor for Canada's two-pin sockets.

WEATHER IN VANCOUVER

High season
Low season

	JAN	FEB	MARCH	APRIL	MAY	JUNE	JULY	AUG	SEPT	OCT	NOV	DEC
Daytime temperatures	6°	8°	11°	14°	18°	21°	23°	23°	19°	14°	9°	7°
Night-time temperatures	1°	1°	3°	5°	8°	11°	13°	12°	10°	7°	4°	2°
☀ Hours of sunshine per day	2	3	4	6	7	7	9	8	6	4	2	1
🌧 Rainfall days per month	17	13	14	11	7	5	4	7	7	15	16	18
≈ Sea temperatures in °C	8°	7°	8°	9°	11°	13°	14°	14°	13°	12°	11°	10°

☀ Hours of sunshine per day   🌧 Rainfall days per month   ≈ Sea temperatures in °C

HOLIDAY VIBES

FOR RELAXATION & CHILLING

FOR BOOKWORMS & FILM BUFFS

📖 AFTER RIVER

Life on a small farm in Western Canada is idyllic until the charismatic character River turns up, setting in motion a chain of ominous events. Author Donna Milner knows exactly how to build up the tension. A great 400-page book which you won't be able to put down (2008).

📖 UNDER DARK WATERS

How and why did her husband die in a seaplane crash? Protagonist Sonja is on a mission to find the truth. A gripping journey through British Columbia written by Bernadette Calonego (2007).

📖 THE SWARM

German author Frank Schätzing did a lot of research for his 1,000-page eco-thriller with a deep-ocean theme that is set on the Pacific coast by Vancouver Island (2004).

🎥 FORSAKEN

2015 saw the release of the first movie in which the two Canadian superstars Donald and Kiefer Sutherland star together. The film features the era of the gunslingers in the prairie and mountains of Alberta around 1870.

PLAYLIST

0:58

‖ **HEAD ABOVE WATER – AVRIL LAVIGNE**
Hypnotic sounds by the megastar who made a comeback after a long break

▶ **SUMMER OF 69 – BRYAN ADAMS**
A powerful classic by the Canadian star

▶ **OBLIVION – GRIMES**
Electro-pop by a promising young Canadian artist

▶ **DOWN TO MY LAST CIGARETTE – K D LANG**
Country feeling from the most famous voice in Alberta

▶ **TAKE BACK THIS LAND – CHILLIWACK**
Hit by the Western Canadian rock band

The holiday soundtrack is available at **Spotify** under **MARCO POLO** Canada

Or scan the code with the Spotify app

ONLINE

@GEORGIASTRAIGHT
Get the latest news on Twitter from Vancouver's city newspaper. The associated website offers plenty of other topics about nightlife, art, ice hockey and restaurants plus blogs and videos.

INDIGENOUSBC.COM
The history and traditions of the First Nations in British Columbia. Special offers for tourists and numerous tips on lodges, canoe tours and cultural centres.

PARKS CANADA NATIONAL APP
App for iPhone and Android with descriptions of the individual nature reserves, hiking trails and YouTube videos. The website features special pages on animal migrations, geocaching, etc.

YUKONQUEST.INFO
Website of the longest and toughest dog-sled race in the North.

TRAVEL PURSUIT

THE MARCO POLO HOLIDAY QUIZ

Do you know what makes Western Canada tick? Test your knowledge of the vast region's customs and quirks. You will find the answers at the foot of the page, with more detailed explanations on pages 18–23.

❶ Why did the First Nations on the west coast carve totem poles?
a) As ostentatious and prestigious objects
b) For tying up prisoners before burning them at the stake
c) As a religious symbol, venerated on holy days

❷ How tall do Douglas fir trees grow?
a) 65m
b) 80m
c) 94m

❸ A well-known Canadian pop singer's name sounds like
a) A hoofed animal that feeds on bog plants
b) A rodent that constructs dams
c) A predator that lives in packs

❹ How much land is protected in Canada's national parks?
a) 1.2 times the area of the United Kingdom
b) Three times the area of the UK
c) Six times the area of Ireland

❺ Who is Canada's head of state?
a) Prime Minister Justin Trudeau
b) Queen Elizabeth II
c) Prince Charles

Mackenzie Delta

❻ Who invented ice hockey as a sport?
a) Dutch people on the frozen tidal flats during the Little Ice Age around 1650
b) The Americans at the Niagara Falls around 1750
c) The sailors of the Franklin Expedition in the Arctic around 1850

❼ What is the Canadian Prime Minister's hobby?
a) Ice hockey
b) Salmon fishing in the wilderness
c) Boxing

❽ What activities are allowed in national parks?
a) Picking flowers on the mountain meadows at the end of the summer
b) Feeding the bears when they emerge from their caves in the spring
c) Fishing for trout in the emerald-green lakes in high summer

❾ What is the likely reason for the increased populations of bark beetles in the forests of Western Canada?
a) Global warming, because beetles like warm weather
b) Monocultures – the First Nations only ever planted pine trees
c) The beetles are spread across the country on tourists' boots

INDEX

CREDITS

Credits
Cover Picture: ABanff National Park, Moraine Lake (AWL images: M. Colombo)
Photos: DuMont Bildarchiv: F. Heuer (front flap outside, front flap inside, back flap, 1, 43, 152/153), Hicker (18, 23, 57, 111); G. Hartmann (112); huber-images: P. Canali (6/7, 102/103), G. Simeone (68), M. Verin (128/129); Laif: Hub (11); Laif/hemis.fr (9); mauritius images/age (34/35, 44, 89); mauritius images/age fotostock/Hoffmann Photography (28); mauritius images/Alamy (10, 24/25, 27, 32/33, 72/73, 84/85, 95, 107, 108, 115, 126, 139, 154/155), M. Bruxelle (144/145), Y. Cardozo (31), R. Chua (116/117), M. DeFreitas (30/31), H. Georgi (100), C. Harris (71), T. Ho (77), P. Horsley (47), D. Kleyn (2/3), J. Koreski (136), Nalidsa (74), M. P. O'Neill (59, 60), R. Sawangphon; (131), M. Smart (8), F. van Wijk (12/13), H. M. Weidman (78), S. Winter (80/81); mauritius images/Alamy/All Canada Photos (62/63); mauritius images/Alamy/sixshooter (147); mauritius images/Alamy/travel4pictures (38/39); mauritius images/Alamy/travelstock44: J. Held (26/27); mauritius images/Alaska Stock: K. Smith (83); mauritius images/Axiom Photographic (14/15); mauritius images/Danita Delimont/Jaynes: M. Grandmaison (21); mauritius images/Firstlight (50/51); mauritius images/Imagebroker: N. Eisele-Hein (97), J. Pfatschbacher (93), E. Strigl (125), S. Wackerhagen (118/119, 123, 142); mauritius images/Travel Collection (48); mauritius images/Westend61/ Fotofeeling (64/65); T. Stankiewicz (98); K. Teuschl (135, 159); Shutterstock/Chase Clausen (158)

4th Edition – fully revised and updated 2022
Worldwide Distribution: Heartwood Publishing Ltd, Bath, United Kingdom
www.heartwoodpublishing.co.uk

© MAIRDUMONT GmbH & Co. KG, Ostfildern
Authors: Karl Teuschl
Editors: Marlis v. Hessert-Fraatz
Picture editor: Ina-Marie Inderka
Cartography: © MAIRDUMONT, Ostfildern (pp. 36–37, 130, 134, 138, 143, outer flap, pull-out map) DuMont Reisekartografie, Fürstenfeldbruck © MAIRDUMONT, Ostfildern (p. 91, 96)
© MAIRDUMONT, Ostfildern, using data from OpenStreetMap, Licence CC-BY-SA 2.0 (pp. 40–41, 52–53, 55, 66–67, 86–87, 104–105, 109, 120–121).
Cover, wallet and pull-out map design: bilekjaeger_Kreativagentur with Zukunftswerkstatt, Stuttgart
Page design: Langenstein Communication GmbH, Ludwigsburg

Heartwood Publishing credits:
Translated from the German by Wendy Barrow, Lindsay Chalmers-Gerbracht, Rupert Kindermann and Thomas Moser
Editors: Felicity Laughton, Kate Michell, Sophie Blacksell Jones
Prepress: Summerlane Books, Bath
Printed in India

MARCO POLO AUTHOR
KARL TEUSCHL

Bears and whales are Karl's passion, as is the vastness of Canada – its enormous, unspoilt landscapes where people have not yet left their mark. Author and filmmaker Karl Teuschl lives in Vancouver and is the North America correspondent for German travel magazine *GEO-Saison1*. He travels through Canada several times a year in search of new and exciting topics!

DOS & DON'TS

HOW TO AVOID SLIP-UPS & BLUNDERS

DON'T UNDERESTIMATE DISTANCES

Distances can be deceiving, especially in the vast north of the country where the width of a finger on the map can mean a long day trip on seemingly endless dirt roads.

DO NOTIFY AUTHORITIES BEFORE GOING ON A HIKE

Before setting off into the wilderness, leave a note with your route and the time of your return with canoe rentals, bush pilots that take you into the hinterland or park wardens. Police stations (RCMP) also accept these notes. If something does go wrong, a search party can be sent out. Don't forget to report back after your return.

DO SCARE OFF THE BEARS

Bears have an excellent sense of smell, but their eyesight is poor. If you are out walking upwind and surprise a bear, they will be aggressive. When hiking, it is best to talk loudly, sing or wear a bell on your leg so that you announce your presence and give any bears in the area time to move away.

DON'T DRIVE UNDER THE INFLUENCE OF ALCOHOL

The limit is 0.8. In the event of an accident the insurance company will not pay out if you are over the limit. The police have no tolerance for drink drivers and there are tough penalties.

DON'T FEED THE MOSQUITOES

The biggest mistake is to hike in the Canadian wilderness without mosquito protection. Remedies such as Off, Muskol or Cutter keep the little bloodsuckers away. The buzzing monsters are particularly active in early summer, but at least they don't transmit any diseases.